C000162136

FRONT COVER - SSgt David Hamel with SR-71 at Offutt Air Force Base Airshow, Nebraska, 1982
TITLE PAGE - A1C David Hamel with F-15A ejection seat at Bitburg Air Base, West Germany, 1978
BACK COVER - SSgt David Hamel at Patrick Air Force Base, Florida, 1983

MY COLD WAR LIFE

THREE DECADES OF SILENT BATTLE

David Hamel

Printed in the United States of America
Library of Congress Control Number: 2023903886
ISBN: Softcover   979-8-88963-175-0
         e-Book   979-8-88963-176-7

Republished by: PageTurner Press and Media LLC
Publication Date: 05/25/2023

To order copies of this book, contact:
PageTurner Press and Media
Phone: 1-888-447-9651
info@pageturner.us
www.pageturner.us

CONTENTS

PREFACE AND TERMS

In writing "My Cold War Life," I wanted to reflect upon and understand my life in the context of ideologies during my early years of growing up in the 1960s through my teenage years into the 1970s. These formative years transitioned into a decision to join the United States Armed Forces and into the Cold War environments in which I would serve during the 1980s. I joined the Air Force delayed enlistment program inactive reserves on 22 December 1976 and converted to active duty on 1 July 1977. I would go on to serve 30 years before retiring in 2007 … that covers a lot of military history since the end of the Vietnam War in 1975. But, I chose to limit this writing to the Cold War era since I have previously covered most of my post-Cold War military story in two other books that I have authored, albeit in entirely different settings. In "4:09 to 9:02" Boston to Oklahoma and New York Cities: Beyond the Bombings, and "TRIFECTA" 26+ Years of 26.2: Chronicles of a Marathoner, much of my military service background is generally overviewed from after Operation "Desert Storm" in 1991, onward.

But prior to 1991, the world was a much different place during those nuclear-fearing days as well as the concept of Mutual Assured Destruction (MAD) between the two superpowers at the time, the Soviet Union and the United States. If you lived during the second half of the Cold War, perhaps you can relate to some of these snapshots in time. If you have not lived during those times perhaps you will gain some insight and understanding of it and of the Cold War that was quietly fought and won. Like the patriotic World War I song of 1917 by George M. Cohen, many of us believed it was best to keep the fight, "Over There." It was part of the U.S. Military policy of "containment" of preventing the spread of communism. Wall and borders really mattered … on land, sea, and air. Those times served as a bridge to the freedoms we enjoy today. Let us drift back in time … together!

(Shutterstock)

Marxism–The political, economic, and social theories of Karl Marx including the belief that the struggle between social classes is a major force in history and that there should eventually be a society in which there are no classes

Marxism-Leninism–a theory and practice of communism developed by Lenin from doctrines of Marx

Socialism–**1.** any of various economic and political theories advocating collective or governmental ownership and administration of the means of production and distribution of goods. **2.a.** a system of society or group living in which there is no private property. **2.b.** a system or condition of society in which the means of production are owned and controlled by the state. 3. a stage of society in Marxist theory transitional between capitalism and communism and distinguished by unequal distribution of goods and pay according to work done

Communism–**1.a.** a system in which goods are owned in common and are available to all as needed. **1.b.** a theory advocating elimination of private property. **2.A** a doctrine based on revolutionary Marxian socialism and Marxism-Leninism that was the official ideology of the U.S.S.R.

Totalitarianism–a system of government that is centralized and dictatorial and requires complete subservience to the state

Capitalism–**1**. an economic system, characterized by private or corporate ownership of capital goods, by investments that are determined by private decision, and by prices, production, and the distribution of goods that are determined mainly by competition in a free market

Free Enterprise–an economic system in which private business operates in competition and largely free of state control

www.merriam-webster.com/dictionary
(accessed 12 December 2021)

THE COLD WAR

The Cold War was a constant state of hostility between the United States and the Union of Soviet Socialist Republics known as the U.S.S.R. or Soviet Union. The Soviet Union was comprised of Russia and its satellite countries of Eastern Europe. It began in 1947 shortly after the end of World War II and continued through the end of the 1980s. During this time, the Soviets were expanding their influence over east Europe after the fall of Nazi Germany. Most notably starting with the Berlin Blockade in 1948 and 1949 and the follow-on formation of communist bloc countries. With the fall of Imperial Japan in 1945 came the withdrawal of Japanese forces from Korea and Vietnam. In addition, China's follow-on civil war resulted in its mainland becoming a communist nation in 1949 forcing the Republic of China leadership to retreat to the island of Taiwan. Attempting to unite under fair and free elections were not successful as communist entities tried to unite by force leading to the Korean War from 1950 to 1953. Similar events led to the French Indo-China War from 1946 to 1954, which became the Vietnam War (Vietnam, Laos, and Cambodia) from 1955 to 1975. With the fall of the Berlin Wall in 1989, and the follow-on collapse of the Soviet Union, the 42-year Cold War effectively came to a close in 1991.

Although I was born in 1959, I grew up during the 1960s and 1970s. Vietnam was a war that got the most daily attention. But in its totality, with the associated Marxism and socialism ideologies, I always understood the Cold War as a "Global War on Communism." But this Global War on Communism was a concept that I accepted early which enabled me to see the separate wars, skirmishes, and conflicts as interrelated and not separate incidents. For me, this understanding was a key factor during my formative years of how I saw the world and where I would fit in with my American upbringing. The absence of this understanding being communicated well enough in our education system, I believe, was a major factor contributing to the unpopularity of the Vietnam War and general national confusion. Despite the political climate of its time, the frequent disconnection from World War II was equally disappointing. But for those of us who could see the "big picture," it sure made understanding the history, sacrifices, and costs of freedom much easier to acknowledge … and that the "torch of freedom" had been handed over to me and the next generation of veterans that would follow.

Perhaps you may recognize this sign growing up. They had been placed on various public and private buildings designating them as a fall-out shelter. In July of 1961, President Kennedy gave a speech about a national safety plan. And so the Office of Civil Defense (which later became FEMA, the Federal Emergency Management Agency) set criteria to protect against radioactive fallout (and not so much the blast itself). Thus, a protection factor of at least 40 was set. That is, you would receive 1/40th of the radiation inside a building versus being unprotected outside. It also had to be roomy enough for 50 people allowing for 10 square feet of space per person. By the mid-1960s, Boston alone had 2,000 such buildings identified and over 1,000 of them had been marked with these iconic black and yellow signs. This information is derived from an article by Edgar B. Herwick III of GBH News - Boston (January 23, 2018). He interviewed a citizen historian named Sean Colby who attended a middle school in Boston when he was young and questioned the history of the signs.

(Creative Commons)

As I was born and raised in Springfield, Massachusetts during the John F. Kennedy (JFK) presidential time, there was a lot of news exposure of the President since it was his home state as well. He was born in Brookline near Boston, and like I, was of the Catholic faith. In essence, my Cold War life story really begins with him …

As a Boy Scout in 1970 With JFK Tapestry on Wall

BABY BOOMERS

I was also part of the "Baby Boomer" Generation, essentially those of us born between 1946 and 1964. There are all kinds of statistics and associations made about "Boomers" but for me it was still about black and white camera photos and TVs (with the "rabbit ear" antennas with aluminum foil). As young as I was, I still vividly remember sitting on my dad's lap on that sad November day in 1963 when President Kennedy was assassinated, with the follow-on funeral procession images on the TV. The assassin, Lee Harvey Oswald, was a U.S. Marine veteran who defected to the Soviet Union and was a self-acknowledged communist who later returned to the U.S. My parents were visibly shocked and upset as the nation greatly mourned his death and I absorbed their emotional reactions. But Kennedy's vision and actions of those times would have significant impact on the nation and my life. The Gary Powers U-2 shoot-down incident of 1960, the Cuban Missile Crisis of 1962, and the Apollo space missions of the late 1960s that led to landing a man on the moon in 1969, were huge national events. These were major tone-setters for the rest of the Cold War. These events would have an influence on me during my military career some 15 to 20 years later.

As a late Boomer, I also believed I had retained many of the carry-over values of my parents and grandparents of the World War II era. Despite the "sex, drugs, and rock 'n roll" social activity that was quickly growing and leading up to the Woodstock Festival in New York in 1969, America was still a vastly traditional conservative-oriented nation. Political parties rarely strayed away from the concept of "God and country." During JFK's inauguration speech in January of 1961, he inspired a nation with, "Ask not what your country can do for you, but what you can do for your country." As a Boomer, I appreciated the sacrifices of military service. JFK was a Navy veteran and war hero. When his patrol torpedo boat (PT-109) was rammed by a Japanese destroyer in World War II, he survived and saved most of his crew with his swimming skills. He was also the first president to have been a Boy Scout … two traits that I aspired to emulate.

My Dad, Raymond Hamel, My Brother Ronald, and Myself, at JFK Gravesite; Spring 1964

Also With My Mom, Helen Hamel, at Arlington National Cemetery

For Boomers, the competition with the Soviet Union in space was a motivating force. It drove JFK to propose that the U.S. should commit itself, "… before the decade is out, of landing a man on the moon and returning him safely to earth." We would think big as a nation and in July of 1969, Commander Neil Armstrong would do just that. I remember when my neighbor's grandfather called his grandson Jimmy and I to go inside his house. He insisted that we watch the moon landing on his black and white TV set, and showed how excited he was. He explicitly told us that we are witnessing the hugest American accomplishment of our lifetime … thinking big, setting goals, and achieving them were hallmarks of this generation. |And Neil Armstrong was also an Eagle Scout! Wow, an Eagle Scout on the moon … "one small step for man, one giant leap for mankind." That really resonated with me.

But by the early 1970s the Vietnam War and the rebellious era loomed largely in the forefront of the political landscape. The Kent State University shootings of 13 unarmed students by Ohio National Guardsman during an anti-war peace rally in May 1970 fueled more anti-military sentiment. The mandatory military draft of the time was replaced with the all-volunteer military in 1973. This was accompanied by an oil embargo, long gas lines, and odd-even day fill-ups if you could get it. The resignation of President Richard Nixon in 1974 compounded the chaos of the times. Although the war would end in 1975, by extension, my teen years would be caught up in these tumultuous political settings continuing into my high school years. These would prove to be very socially unpopular and highly frowned upon attitudes towards graduates like me who decided to join the military. But, growing up on Calhoun Street in our old late 1890s house with Mom, Dad and brother Ronald were much simpler times. We celebrated early life events such as my First Holy Communion after church, Easter, and various religious and national holidays.

Our Late-1890s Era House

But as a group, Boomers are generally considered wealthy, active, and somewhat of a physically fit generation. We grew up expecting the world to improve with time. We still believe we are a special generation and worked hard expecting to reap success from our labor. We are the first to define the world in terms of generations. But I have been very fortunate and appreciative to have had personal access to a few World War I veterans and many World War II "Greatest Generation" veterans and Post-War cohorts. Meeting many heroes of those times while they were alive are still very special memories to me.

New heroes constantly emerge but are fewer in numbers and harder to access. Worse yet, they are lesser known today or appreciated in the follow-on generations … they have generally taken a back seat to entertainment stars. But there are many heroes out there that still impact my life today. As such, this writing is a testament to them.

SERVICE INFLUENCERS

Growing up during my Cold War life also featured several family members and close personal associations who served in the military. All would be positive influencers on me as I explored the military service option before high school graduation. Service, sacrifice, pride, and even health issues would all be variables to consider, especially in light of the unpopularity of the Vietnam War.

My father served in the Army in the 82nd Airborne as a Korea War-era veteran from 1953 to 1955. He was a paratrooper and a jeep driver with a mounted recoilless gun and completed jungle training in Panama.

My parents gave me my middle name of "Leo" in honor of my late Uncle Leo Hamel who served in the Navy during the Korean War. He later served in the Springfield, Massachusetts Police Department and was killed in the line of duty in 1955. His badge was retired in bronze during a memorial monument unveiling at the SPD on 3 May 1987. His name is also carved in the wall at the National Law Enforcement Memorial in Washington D.C. (pane 5E, line 5).

Living up to the honor of him and his name was a huge influencer and had significant impact as I lived my life. Ironically, I would run in an "End of Watch" 13.1 mile Half-Marathon (virtual) for fallen police officers in his honor in January 2021, some 65 years later!

It is notable that he was posthumously awarded the Medal of Honor by the Springfield, Massachusetts Police Department presented to his widow, Mrs. Beverly Hamel. The medal, made of solid gold, was inscribed as:

"Leo G. Hamel, for valor, Department of Police, Springfield, Mass." On the backside is the inscription, "who valiantly in the performance of his duty gave his life to prevent death to others."

Article and Medal Adapted From an Old Newspaper Clipping,
Probably a Local Springfield, Ma Paper in 1955

"Officer Hamel was killed in the line of duty when he was crushed between two vehicles while attempting to stop a vehicle from being driven by a patient with mental health issues. Officer Hamel jumped onto the running board of the vehicle, but was killed when the vehicle sideswiped a second vehicle. Officer Hamel was 26 years old, serving with the Springfield Police Department for 3 years."

Springfieldmapolice.com – fallen officers

My father's brother, my Uncle Jean-Paul Hamel, served over 20 years in the Massachusetts Air National Guard in aircraft maintenance as an aircraft crew chief. In many aspects, I followed my uncle in the same career path with much time around aircraft on the flight line.

My mother's sister, Pauline Cote's husband, Uncle Raymond Cote, served in the Air Force in the 1950s as an electronics technician.

My father's oldest sister Theresa's husband, Uncle Edgar Gionet, served in the U.S. Marine Corps during World War II in the Pacific during the Battle of Cape Gloucester on the island of New Britain, a territory of New Guinea. He served with the 3rd Battalion, 5th Regiment, K Company, of the 1st Marine Division (nicknamed Dark Horse). He was wounded in the left arm by a Japanese sniper on 2 January 1944. He went to Brisbane, Australia for rest and recuperation then separated as a Lance Corporal. He earned a Purple Heart medal for being combat wounded from that engagement. He survived the war and raised a family. He quietly showed me his medal twice when I asked him about it. Yes, that had an inspiring impact on this young boy ... duty and sacrifice.

My father's second sister Yvonne's husband, Uncle Matthew Salvato, served in the Army Air Forces during the Korean War. He was a radio maintenance technician on B-29 Superfortresses.

My father's youngest sister Rita's husband married Matthew Salvato's brother, Uncle Michael Salvato, who served in the Navy during the Korean War on an aircraft carrier. He was very active in his church with the California Knights of Columbus as a State Color Corps Commander.

My Uncle Mathew Salvato's son, my cousin Roger Salvato, served in the Navy as a rate construction technician, E-5, in a construction battalion (CB). Known as "Seabees," he served in Vietnam from 1966 to 1968 at forward bases at Chi Lai, Phu Bai, and Hue.

Aside from family members, my Boy Scout facility manager Francis "Buck" Rogers served in the Army in World War II. "Bucky" often talked with pride about being in charge of many military supply warehouses in the Philippine Islands. He hired me as a landscaper, my first job.

A bartender at Kip's Café down on Main street in Springfield, "Skippy" Remillard (no photo), served in the Navy during the Korean War. He would stare at me with his arms crossed as he puffed on his stubby cigar. But this "old salt" had a big influence on me and really was a deciding factor when I was "on the fence" about joining the Air Force. Although the drinking age in Massachusetts at the time was 18, I regularly got served at several bars at 17. After work on school nights, I would pop in for a "night cap" beer (quite customary at the time even at my young age). He would talk to me as I told him my plans and he encouraged me to join the service and not "dead-end" at the bars as he'd seen too many people do.

There were certainly many others who had served and influenced me over my early years, particularly my Scoutmaster Leo J. Maynard, who was also a Korean War veteran (no photo). He was very Catholic oriented and I attended all his Bible sessions associated with my Ad Altare Dei religious medal Boy Scout award. That said, I was never fearful of older folks and was never afraid to seek their advice or council especially in the Scouting world … and yes, most of them were veterans. Often the pubs and quiet bars provided some of the access to these old warriors. The Bancroft Café bar also on Main Street was a quiet smoky place that Bucky and the old-timers would frequent. A couple other places that I would frequent were the Glenwood Café on Springfield Street in Springfield and the Polish American Veterans club in Chicopee, Massachusetts. My humble gratitude to them all!

RAISED 1960s

My Mom and Dad, Raymond and Helen Hamel raised four children on Calhoun Street in Springfield. I was the oldest and my brother Ronald was born a year later. There was an eight year gap as my sister Lisa was born in 1969 and my youngest brother Eric came along a year after her. We all grew up in Springfield and started kindergarten at Jefferson Street School then we eventually went to school at Saint Thomas Aquinas, and its same-named Catholic church adjacent to it. In the 1960s, I was schooled by Catholic nuns wearing the traditional black habits. We lived in a French-speaking Canadian community so the nuns knew and taught French. Aside from English, Masses were also in French and in Latin. The nuns were tough and kept us well disciplined. Because of that discipline, we learned very well. It was very "old school" indeed. I vividly remember the old ink-well type desks that we used, the old black and white composition books to write in, and the screechy black chalk boards.

During these years, I underwent the religious sacrament process as I was baptized on 19 April 1959, received 1st Holy Communion on 11 May 1967 and was Confirmed in 1970. For Catholics, the Sacrament of Confirmation is important because as a teenager we receive the Holy Spirit and become a "Soldier of Christ" as full members of the church and be strengthened in spiritual life. As I entered into adulthood this helped cement my Christian foundations and was a source of strength to overcome life's challenges that were most certainly to come, and as a moral compass to guide me when I needed direction. I became an Altar Boy and assisted in over 80 church services, sang on the Christmas choir team, and often assisted services for Father Gosselin and later Father Chocquette from 1969 through 1973.

During this time, I served in the Knights of the Altar Society (K of A) and advanced through three of its four service stages of Page, Knight, and Knight Commander (the fourth was Grand Knight). The K of A was first organized in the United States in 1938 to organize Altar boys into a society to assist priests especially during and after the World War II years when men went to war. Prior to this, the Order of the Acolyte within seminaries performed many of these duties as a step to the goal of priesthood. Although the first altar servers were formed in Italy in the late 1850s, in past centuries only priests or those ordained to the office of Acolyte were allowed beyond the Communion's serving rail. After the Second Vatican Council closed in 1965 the traditional Latin mass began to die out and with it the K of A in the United States. Essentially, I was part of that dying out period, some of which would reemerge later under Pope John Paul II. But the nearness to serving with priests at the altar: march in procession into a full-house church, the lighting of candles, holding an open Bible as the priest read from it, handling a chalice, ringing the bells, and washing of the hands, were all very prestigious and honorable services to perform, all in front of an often packed congregation. In America, it was very common for churches of various denominations to have active youth groups, Bible studies, or support organizations and programs … not so in most communist countries. Most of America's faiths were based on, and very much in line with, traditional Judeo-Christian values.

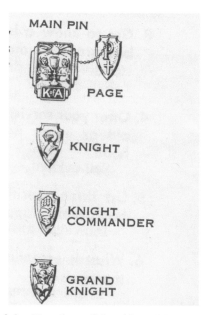

(Constitution of the Knights of the Altar, Notre Dame, IN, 1966)

While at St Thomas, I participated in several Trick-or-Treat for UNICEF fund-raising programs for children. Sponsored by the United Nations Children's Fund (UNICEF), I solicited for monetary donations in small orange boxes from door-to-door house visits. We were taught the virtues of being a volunteer and to help the less fortunate. Being involved in our community and support charitable groups such as Catholic Charities were public obligations of basic citizenship and of being an American … and yes we recited the Pledge of Allegiance with our right hand over our heart every morning to start the day followed by a prayer; usually an "Our Father" followed by a "Hail Mary." Every classroom had an American flag on a pole attached to the wall, always.

I also served as a "Patrol Boy" or school crosswalk guard at street crossings wearing reflective white belts to safely escort students when school finished for the day. I also loved to read and would often chase down the local travelling Bookmobile to sign-out books. I rode my bicycle all the time and frequented the Springfield library, museum, planetarium, and historical landmarks (Springfield Armory, Chapin Monument, Old Day House, etc). My friends and I all knew how to change a bicycle tire tube and replace the sprocket chain. We were physically active all the time. In New England we ice skated and played pond hockey in the winter. We also could throw a baseball or a football. Since my hometown of Springfield was the birthplace of basketball and home of the Basketball Hall of Fame, that sport was also played often … and throughout the 1960s the Boston Celtics had won eight straight NBA Championships. But no matter the sport, you had to be home before the street lights came on!

Street Light (Behind Tree) On Calhoun Street 1967

Neil Armstrong (Eagle Scout)

(Shutterstock)

TEENS: 1970s

By the early 1970s, I was a teenager and got involved with Boy Scouting. I was very active in my local Troop 14 in Springfield. I advanced through the positions of Assistant Patrol Leader, Patrol Leader, Quartermaster, Senior Patrol Leader, Scribe, and Junior Assistant Scoutmaster. My activities and involvement included Project SOAR (Save Our American Resources) cleaning up polluted riverbanks, community park repairs, and aluminum and newspaper recycling efforts in 1970 and 1971. I served as a personal altar server and as a Chaplain's Aide for a district boy scout chaplain, conducting church services at scout camps throughout Western Massachusetts. I was awarded the Gold Quill Award in 1972 for outstanding journalism, reporting, photography, and communication then awarded the Ad Altare Dei Catholic Religious Medal in 1973. I served as a Den Chief for Cub Scout activities in 1973 and 1974 and led troop participation of basketball tournaments with the mentally challenged in Belchertown, Massachusetts in 1974.

I completed a Troop Leadership Development Course (TLDC) at Camp Woronoak, Massachusetts in July 1975 and sold chocolate bars to fund and participate in large state scout summer camporees in 1975 and 1976. I completed 33 merit badges and 6 skill awards and earned Tenderfoot, Second Class, First Class, Star, and Life Scout. Culminating this, was with the top rank of Eagle Scout in 1975 with a Bronze Palm in 1976 (for 5 additional merit badges beyond requirements) … and my Eagle Scout Award card was signed by President Gerald Ford who was also an Eagle Scout! I could now fall in good company of only two Presidents that were Boy Scouts … both in my lifetime. Of course, the other president was John F. Kennedy who reached the level of Star Scout. Neil Armstrong was very much on my mind as an Eagle Scout too. I even met my first girlfriend, known to me as "Rhiannon" or "Rhi," at my Eagle Scout banquet in the food serving line! Even she as a server participated in events. That was one thing I always appreciated and admired growing up … always meeting and being associated with people who were doing something positive in the community, no matter how small it might be. To me it was about the concept of active citizenship during the Cold War that was something to be proud of. JFK and his "Ask not" speech felt alive and well!

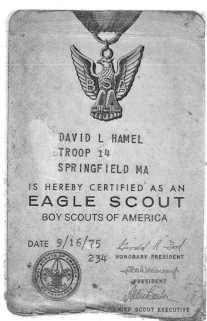

From 1972 to 1975, my first real job was as a landscaper. I maintained large front, back, and side yards at a Syrian-Lebanese American Club in Springfield (also home to Boy Scout Troop 14). I mowed yards, trimmed trees, pruned bushes, raked leaves, and shoveled snow and was paid by the club caretaker. I was also a masonry apprentice loading and unloading bricks, cement bags, tools, & equipment for Armand Roy Contractor, mainly as a summer hire. I helped build brick fireplaces and mixed and poured concrete patios and driveways in Southwick, Massachusetts and Enfield, Connecticut. During my teen years my friends all worked and learned skills and trades early in life. When we got our first cars we learned how to maintain them as best we could. Everyone wanted muscle cars of the late '60s. We loved getting our hands dirty and trying to figure how things operated. My first car was a 1967 Ford Country Squire station wagon. A rust-bucket that was a real beater, but it got me to school and work!

I went to Roger L. Putnam Vocational Technical High School in 1973 and began learning the heating and air conditioning trade. For extracurricular high school activity I joined the Drama Club and learned on-stage acting. I participated in mainly Shakespeare plays such as Hamlet and Romeo & Juliet. I also played intramural floor hockey as a goalie and won its indoor school championship in 1976. I also worked as a janitor and operated buffers, large Zamboni-type floor machines, and greased laundry cart wheel bearings for Richco Janitor Services. It was at Massachusetts Mutual Life Insurance Company in Springfield after school for 4 hours on weeknights. A huge building with many offices, it was good entry-level job and located right across the street from the high school.

Through all my myriad of activities, I was very athletic and swam with various swimming teams with the Springfield Boy's Club from 1970 to 1972 (and also remembering JFK as a swimmer). I also played street hockey and started out in yard scrimmages then played in various neighborhood pickup games in all positions. This led to playing high school level ice hockey starting in 1972 with the Brightwood Blazers team (Springfield, MA) where I led the inner-city league's defenseman in goal-scoring (10 goals) in 1975. I also played on the Springfield Flyers team in 1976 & 1977. I was also quite the sprinter during our daily "cafeteria dash" hallway races to be first in line … and I often won! I was also a passionate model-builder and assembled and painted many World War II airplane, ship, and tank models. This greatly enhanced my grades on book reports that were associated with these projects while at St Thomas. Following detailed assembly instructions enabled me to develop my attention to detail. It also developed my manual dexterity skills that also applied to learning the heating and air conditioning trade skills in high school and beyond.

In the backdrop of growing up in the '60s and '70s, I always remembered looking up and watching the tall-tail B-52C and D model bombers and KC-135A tankers circling over our house in their pattern flying in and out of nearby Westover Air Force Base in Chicopee, Massachusetts which was home of the 99th Bombardment Wing. These long-range aircraft armed with nuclear devices were kept on continuous alert at various bases as part of the Strategic Air Command's (SAC) massive retaliation strategy during the Cold War. Also, many of the SAC crews were sent to Vietnam on B-52 bombing missions … and of course this fed the anti-war protests at the base gate that was frequently covered in the news. These served as reminders of the times as well as the Civil Defense siren tests and drills. But soon enough at 17, I would be thinking about joining the military.

BECOMING AN AIRMAN

During this time, the images of the Huey helicopter lifting off the roof of the U.S. Embassy in Saigon in April of 1975 marked the sad ending of the Vietnam War for America. The images of its aftermath of more than a million refugees fleeing Vietnam mostly by boat and many that died was also covered on the news. Of the 58,220 Americans killed in the War 1,335 were from Massachusetts. Of those, 102 were from Hampden County, and 48 were from my hometown of Springfield (as listed on the Springfield 50 Project, Western Massachusetts Vietnam Veterans Memorial). During my high school years after President Nixon, President Gerald Ford stabilized the country during tumultuous times through the election of 1976.

As I entered my high school senior year of 1977, I knew I couldn't afford going to college financially, but I did have a trade. By this time my girlfriend Rhiannon (that I met at my Eagle Scout Award banquet in 1975) and I were engaged. Trying to plan a future after graduation was difficult. But in the '70s this was a common life path for many … get married and go to work or college. I also knew that we needed a clean break away from Springfield to start a new life. I believed the military was my best option. Although very unpopular at the time, I went to visit a military recruiter. I knew the Air Force was for me especially with my fascination of aircraft during my model-making years. A major incentive at the time was that the eligibility for the Vietnam-era G.I. Bill (Government Issue-military term) was expiring on 1 January 1977. At 17, I made the pitch to my parents since they had to sign the application form as I was not yet 18. After some discussion, they approved it. Thus, I entered the Air Force 6-month delayed enlistment program on 22 December 1976, a week prior to its expiration … and little would I know that my Brother Ronald would join the Army some 8 months later.

Classic 70s!

The year 1977 began with Jimmy Carter being sworn-in as President in January. I turned 18 in April and went to Rhi's High School Prom in May. Then we both graduated in June (from different high schools). During this time, I had been jogging and running to get ready for boot camp and built up to a 2-mile loop around my neighborhood, much like the "Rocky" character in gray sweats (and yes, "Eye of the Tiger" was a big hit then)! I became active-duty status on 1 July. My family threw a big farewell party at home then it was off to San Antonio, Texas to Lackland Air Force Base where I reported for Basic Training. As soon as I got off the bus at 2 am with many other "Rainbows" (different colored clothes), we met the Training Instructor (TI) yelling at us as we got off the bus. More shouts came as we got into a semi-military formation with our suitcases and bags … "pick 'em up – put 'em down! Pick 'em up – put 'em down." He continued on, "For the next six weeks, I'm going to be your father, your mother, your sister, your brother … and your worst nightmare! Do you hear me?" We replied with a feeble "yes, Sir" which continued with follow-on "Yes Sirs!" till we got the correct loudness. We then marched over to the World War II era barracks with open bays and bunked down for the night.

Fortunately, this was the Friday of a 4th of July holiday weekend and training would not resume till Tuesday. So our "Rainbow Flight" of about 20 teenagers would sweat it out in the old wooden two-story barracks with a big wall fan on each floor blowing hot air around. We could only march to the local Shoppette store in "elements" of two airman to buy basic items. I also remember watching the fireworks over Lackland from the barracks break area. It would be our last day as "Rainbows" as the next step was haircuts and new green fatigue uniforms. In the meantime, this ole boy from New England was beginning to struggle with the very humid south Texas heat. As an Airman Basic (E-1) "slick-sleeve" - no stripes, training began with early morning PT (physical training) … but I was struggling to stay hydrated and maintain concentration as the long training days ramped up.

By week two, we were having daily inspections. And lo-and-behold I failed a handkerchief inspection. There were six handkerchiefs that had to be neatly and squarely folded. One of mine was "not quite" folded in the required 4" square. It was explained to me that the other "correctly" folded handkerchiefs were now "incorrect" and the one that was not uniform is now "correct." Puzzled at this logic, the penalty was a one-week set back. Shocked and feeling dejected, I was now fearful of not making it through basic training. To make matters worse, I was sent to Flight 3706 that was made up of Southerners. I came from a Flight of New Englanders. We certainly didn't speak the same English and I couldn't understand a word they were saying. Feeling dumb and like I was in another country, I about needed an interpreter! Actually, I was scared feeling like I was being set up for more failure.

To top it off, my new TI Staff Sergeant (SSgt) Dobbs had a heavy Tennessee mountain speak that I could barely decipher. Feeling dumber, he must have asked himself why they sent him a dumb Yankee. The only good thing that happened through all this was that I was to move out of the old barracks and now into a newer dorm, albeit still open bay … but it had air conditioning! This, coupled with being put on salt tablets with increased water in-take, I was beginning to feel physically better and improved my PT effort with much less struggle. Secondly, these southern boys did not know how to operate a floor buffer machine on tile floors and were crashing it into perfectly aligned beds. This greatly frustrated and angered everyone in the bays since it was a major effort using long strings to make sure the beds were perfectly aligned … an inspection item. This was my time to seize the moment! I was a pro at operating floor buffers from my work experience as a janitor at the Mass Mutual building in Springfield. I now took over command of that duty and instantly became a hero of our flight! Apparently, SSgt Dobbs took notice too. He then selected me to be the flight guide-on flag bearer … a lone position out in front of the flight!

Despite the setback, I rebounded as my confidence grew. I figured out the southern speak and taught them boys how to use a buffer. I was also selected to be a Chapel Guide to lead and march a small religious element to church on Sundays. Other guys were now getting yelled at for other infractions. During a uniform inspection, I vividly recall the guy next to me getting chewed out by the TI … "Benson, are you a communist plot trying to piss me off, but it ain't gonna work!" I got to marching well leading the flight with the flight guide-on staff and flag. Graduation day was ever-so-sweet as all the graduating flights lined up during the graduation parade. As we marched down the approach-way making the "bomb-run" toward the "pass-in-review" area where the General, Colonels, and Commanders were, I lowered the guide-on staff and flag to the "present-arms" command position as the flight simultaneously saluted as we marched by. Once we passed by and the General returned the salute, the command of "order-arms" was called and the flight simultaneously lowered their salutes as I raised the guide-on flag. We then marched back to our starting positions. It was done. We had graduated!

During my time at Lackland, airman were matched and selected for a career field job. Since I had completed four years of heating and air conditioning in high school, I had planned on continuing that trade in the Air Force and my chances were very good since I had scored high on the Armed Forces Vocational Aptitude Test (ASVAB) in the mechanical field. But heating and air conditioning jobs had filled up during that one week when I was setback in Basic. I was offered a "by-pass" test to possibly by-pass others for that field. Despite a very good score, the field was just too stacked and I was a bit out of cycle. But other under-manned mechanical field jobs were open. To meet the school training cycle, I was selected to be an Aircrew Egress Systems mechanic … what in the world is an Egress System? Is it some kind of aircraft heating and cooling system? I couldn't get an answer from the TI. He didn't know either. After 3 days in "casual" civilian clothes, and a nice visit to downtown San Antonio, I was sent to a technical school at Chanute Air Force Base in Rantoul, Illinois and scheduled for a nine-week course in Aircrew Egress Systems.

I flew from San Antonio to Chicago then took a bus to Rantoul. The corn fields seemed endless during that long ride to Chanute. I got settled into an old Korean War-era barracks but was quite happy to have my own room with no roommate. We assembled and marched to school and were assigned to the 3371st School Squadron. The school was for the Aerospace Ground Equipment (AGE) course and the Aircrew Egress Systems (Egress) course. AGE was to learn about, maintain, and operate aircraft support equipment such as powered and non-powered items such as generators, air pressure carts, and various maintenance stands. Egress was to learn about aircraft escape systems such as ejection seats, canopies, parachutes and survival kits. I'd be working with explosives too. So what do these have to do with heating and air conditioning? Not a darn thing! Thus, I was to embark on an entirely new career path that I never would have imagined ... well just shy of assembling model airplanes. Maybe I was somehow destined to be here after all!

During this time, I began having dental problems and was having difficulty focusing on my assignments due to tooth and gum aches and pain. I got through the first block of training but failed the second block ... a test I probably should not have taken being on strong pain relievers after a tooth extraction. With all the scheduled dental work, I was setback a block (about 3 weeks). When all was done, I had 3 tooth extractions, 10 fillings, 2 root canals, and miscellaneous cleanings, ex-rays, and consults. In the midst of all this, I had also received a "Dear John" (break-up) letter from my fiancé, Rhiannon. Apparently, some of our friends were putting bad thoughts into her head about military life, of being gone all the time, and leaving Massachusetts. She began re-thinking what a military marriage would mean for her and then had her eyes set on someone else a little closer to home. Of course, this was exactly what we didn't want to do and that was exactly the reason why we were going to pursue a new life elsewhere. At 18 years old, I could somewhat understand ... but we/I had already committed to making it work. Angered and heart-broken, I was demoralized again as all our plans instantly vaporized. I was now alone and fighting for self-preservation.

MEDICAL/DENTAL APPOINTMENT

INSTRUCTIONS
1. Please meet the appointment(s) made for you promptly
2. Bring this slip with you and give it to the appointment clerk.
3. If you are unable to keep this appointment, cancel it at least 24 hours in advance.

I.   IDENTIFICATION DATA

TYPED NAME OF PATIENT (Last - First - Middle Initial)   GRADE
HAMEL DAVID L   AB
ORGANIZATION OR HOME ADDRESS (Include Zip Code)   SSAN   DUTY PHONE
3371

II.   APPOINTMENT DATA

HOUR	DATE	CLINIC	DOCTOR	TELEPHONE NUMBER	DATE ISSUED	VERIFIED
0730	23 Nov	D/C	Stein	2804	16 Nov	MJ

REMARKS   the last of 23 dental appointments
during my 5 months at Chanute

AF FORM 490
APR 70   PREVIOUS EDITIONS WILL BE USED   U.S. GOVERNMENT PRINTING OFFICE: 1975-573-750

A-1 Skyraider

As I struggled through Egress Tech School during the systems concept-and-operations portion of the block training, I did like the exposure to various aircraft. Though much different from my World War II aircraft model types, I was now into Vietnam aircraft types. I was learning the escape systems of the A-1 Skyraider with the "Yankee" extraction system … basically, a spinner-type extractor rocket with pendant lines (a bungy-type cord) attached to the seat where the pilot is pulled versus ejected, thus "yanked" out. We learned the F-4 Phantom and F-106 Delta Dart with the Martin-Baker systems, the F-111 Aardvark capsule system, and the B-52 Stratofortress with the upward and downward systems. Egress Tech School became more interesting as I got to the hands-on portion of training. I enjoyed the various aircraft types and the training simulators that we used, and removing and replacing explosive initiations, thrusters, and rocket catapults. I began to think that I just might like this new career path if I gave it a chance … and make it through the course.

And there were fun times too as my classmates were now my Air Force buddies, and the barracks parties and fun times at the base pizzeria were great stress relievers. I got through my dental work, passed my school tests, and tried to accept the "Dear John" as part of the process. It turned out that I wasn't the only one getting those kind of letters here and I wasn't alone in the heart-break process. Together we began to heart-mend. But as summer turned to fall, the setback meant that I would not be home for Thanksgiving with Rhi as envisioned anyway … it would be winter in time for Christmas at home with family instead. Meanwhile, I did graduate and became a 3-skill level apprentice and received orders for my first duty assignment. I would be going to Bitburg Air Base in West Germany. During this time, the communist were also making gains in Central America and major civil wars erupted. The Panama Canal Treaty was signed in September giving ownership of the canal from the U.S. to Panama, and the Soviet and Allied forces were militarily poised in East and West Germany. We were losing the Cold War … and I was about to walk into it.

Tech School Graduate

Christmas 1977 at Home With My Sister Lisa and Youngest Brother Eric

BITBURG AIR BASE, WEST GERMANY: ARRIVAL, 1978

I took a very long but scenic train ride from Chicago to Springfield. After nearly six months it was so nice to finally be home. I had survived Air Force Basic Training and Technical School and knew I had a chance to make it through an enlistment despite two setbacks. Though still heart-broken about Rhi, I thought it was best not to pursue her while home on leave. I knew I needed to start fresh when I got to Germany and thought best to leave it all behind as originally intended … now that included her too. Meanwhile, my brother Ronald had joined the Army. I guess he figured he needed a new start in life too, and the military gave him that same opportunity, albeit still at a very unpopular time. As it turns out, he would be home in time for the Christmas holidays too … and he also had an assignment to West Germany!

On 1 January 1978, I was promoted to Airman (E-2) and got to sew on my first stripe before leaving home. I flew to Rhein-Main Air Base in West Germany then took the military "White Swan" bus ride to Bitburg. A long scenic drive through the German countryside, the weather stayed cold, overcast, and damp. Bitburg is 30 miles northeast of Luxembourg City in the Eifel Mountain region. My sponsor got me signed in to the 36th Field Maintenance Squadron and set up a room in the squadron dorm (the word *dorm* was a recent transition from the word *barracks*). The rooms were small for four people and had two bunk beds. As the junior guy, I got an upper bunk. I could also see the German workers shoveling coal into the building's storage hopper since coal was used for heat. I was then issued a ration card to get my share of coffee, tobacco, and liquor.

As he took me to the Egress Shop, I was awed by the new F-15 Eagles taking off with their loud afterburners. The last F-4s had recently been replaced a few months earlier. I met the shop chief who was a Master Sergeant (E-7) and the day shift crew who eagerly welcomed me. I was a bit rank shy and not used to being around anyone with more than one stripe. But my first day would not be without incident.

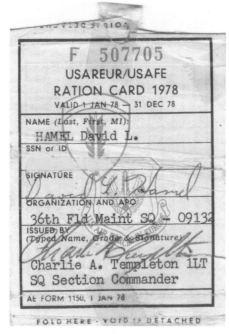

Still in awe, I wanted to see an F-15A Eagle up close. It had big BT letters on the tail designating that it was from Bitburg, home of the 36th Tactical Fighter Wing. The shop was undermanned that day so the shop chief responded to a work order to do a 30-day parachute inspection of a plane in the hangar … and so he took me with him since there was no one else available. He climbed up the ladder, inspected all the safety pins and devices, and kneeled backwards into the ejection seat to be able to perform the parachute inspection. He allowed me to climb up the ladder up to the canopy sill just outside the cockpit to observe. Wow, I was excited to be there on my first non-official job! With the big canopy wide open and all the instruments and gauges crammed together, I had a big smile on my face just standing there. Then suddenly there was a "pop" sound in the cockpit and white silk began to unravel out of the parachute bag. As the shop chief was hugging the parachute trying to minimize its unraveling over the opposite canopy sill, a nearby crew chief observed what was happening and asked me to get down off the ladder so he could assist. He knew something went wrong with a miss-routed ripcord as he saw a six-striper with a popped chute in the cockpit and a one-striper with a big smile standing on the aircraft ladder. The optics were not good. A very embarrassed Master Sergeant and a very ignorant Airman's first time to a jet made for a very memorable first impression and a unique start on Day 1 of my first tour of duty.

The next day I was scheduled to attend the F-15A and B model (two-seater trainer) egress qualification course at the base Field Training Detachment (FTD). The five-day course was much like the egress tech school at Chanute except that it specialized only on the F-15A ESCAPAC IC-7 system. This time there would be no setbacks in training and a happy graduate I was!

(Creative Commons)

Back at the shop, another new Airman would arrive and he and I would become great friends. Lou Irizarry and I were each paired with Staff Sergeants (SSgt, E-5) and went out performing many jobs. As we gained more experience and studied our volumes of Career Development Course (CDCs) we eventually were awarded our 5-skill level. Aside from learning our primary jobs, the base was in a frequent state of exercises and responses. We had our chemical equipment bag with us all the time. In it was a charcoal suit, a gas mask with filters, rubber gloves, and rubber booties, which were difficult to wrap and tie around your boots. When the alarms sounded, we responded to the corresponding sirens, flag colors, and appropriate protective gear to a toxic nuclear, biological, chemical (NBC) threat or attack. We were also issued Atropine auto injectors to combat reactions to chemical nerve agents. This item operated much like an Epinephrine pen (Epipen) for treatment of allergic reaction such as bee stings. It was a spring-loaded needle that was to be injected into the thigh or buttocks with a follow-on 2-PAM injector (for convulsions). These were taken very seriously as we were constantly reminded that the Cold War was still quite hot in Europe.

When World War II ended in 1945, Eastern Europe and the eastern half of Germany were under the control of the Soviet Union and became the Warsaw Pact. Western Europe and the western half of Germany were controlled by the Western Allies and the United States, and became the North Atlantic Treaty Organization (NATO). The former capitol of Germany, Berlin, was divided into four sectors with the Western Allies joining their sectors to form West Berlin while the Soviets held East Berlin. But West and East Berlin were in East Germany (German Democratic Republic or GDR). The Warsaw Pact was established as a balance of power to NATO. Although there was no direct military confrontation among them, the conflict was fought on an ideological basis and in proxy wars in other countries.

STANDARD ALARM SIGNALS		
ALL ATTACKS WIL BE CONSIDERED TO INCLUDE CHEMICALS UNTIL PROVEN OTHERWISE		
SIGNALS	MEANING	ACTIONS
" ALARM YELLOW" (VOICE)	YELLOW ——— ATTACK PROBABLE	YELLOW FIELD GEAR WORN OUTSIDE
YELLOW FLAG (VISUAL)		
UNBROKEN WARBLING ONE MIN DURATION	RED ATTACK IMMINENT ——— IN PROGRESS	RED DON MASKS AND FIELD GEAR. ALL PERSONNEL IMMEDIATELY TAKE COVER; GET IN PRONE POSITION IN A DITCH OR BEHIND A PROTECTIVE OBJECT.
" ALARM RED" (VOICE)		
RED FLAG (VISUAL)		
10 SEC ON, 20 SEC OFF - BROKEN STEADY CONTINUOUS BEATING ON METAL	BLACK WARNING OF IMMINENT ARRIVAL OR PRESENCE OF NBC CONTAMINATION	BLACK DON MASKS AND FIELD GEAR. ALL PERSONNEL, EXCEPT THOSE ENGAGED IN DIRECT MISSION SUPPORT LIFE SAVING ACTIVITIES, GO TO YOUR PROTECTIVE SHELTER
" ALARM BLACK" (VOICE)		
BLACK FLAG (VISUAL)		
"ALL CLEAR" (VOICE)	ALL CLEAR	ALL CLEAR RESUME RECOVERY OPERATIONS
WHITE FLAG (VISUAL)		

(Creative Commons / Cropped)

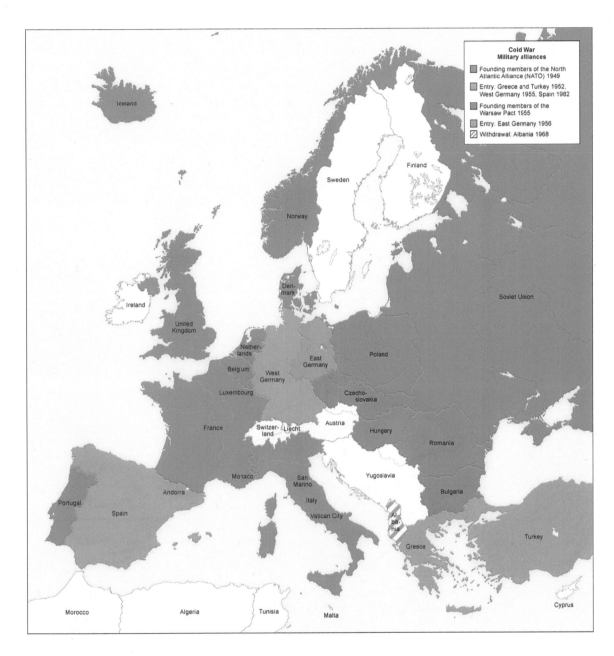

(Creative Commons)

BITBURG AIR BASE, WEST GERMANY, 1978

In 1948, the Soviets blockaded Berlin by sealing off its access corridors. The Western Allies responded with the Berlin Airlift delivering supplies to West Berlin for 15 months. Wanting to avoid open conflict with the West, the Soviets ended the blockade in 1949. But the competing ideological and economic visions for postwar Europe continued. By the early 1960s, many East Germans were fleeing to the west resulting in the East German authorities constructing the Berlin Wall encircling the city. In June of 1963, President Kennedy visited West Berlin challenging Soviet oppression and offered hope to the city with his "Ich bin ein Berliner" (I am a Berliner) speech. Berlin was still at the heart of the Cold War ... and all these years later, Kennedy was still a big part of, and the heart of, me.

In the late 1970s, the Warsaw Pact countries were poised to overrun West Germany through a place called the Fulda Gap. It was one of two avenues that were believed to be routes for a Soviet tank attack from East Germany and the other being at the North German Plain. But the Fulda Gap was a direct advance route to Frankfurt which was the heart of the U.S. military in West Germany and near Rhein-Main Air Base ... both designated to be the main reinforcement receiving areas if war broke out. As such, Exercise "REFORGER" (Return of Forces to Germany) was NATO's annual quick deployment of forces to West Germany from 1969 to 1993 and was the actual plan to strengthen the NATO presence in Europe. It was a huge air, sea, and land effort. In the event of actual conflict it would be renamed Operation "REFORGER." As I supported the air defense effort with the F-15 Eagle, my brother Ronald supported the land defense front as an M-60 Main Battle Tank (MBT) crewman. He often trained at the Grafenwoehr exercise and staging areas. The M-60 was the Army's primary tank during the Cold War. Ronald was also trained and qualified on the M-48 Patton Tank and the M-60 MBT, models A-1 through A-3.

Meanwhile, back at Bitburg the work hours were long, the sirens and exercises were plenty, but the work-hard play-hard ethic was well in place. At the end of many 12-hour shifts a cold beer was the greatest of rewards, and back at the dorms the parties were nightly. Of course that meant frequent bar-hopping raids in downtown Bitburg as well. After all, Bitburg had its own brewery, therefore a taste for Bitburger Pilsener was quickly developed.

In April of '78, I celebrated my 19th birthday downtown and made my way around various German discos and "gasthaus" restaurant pubs. As such, my buddies and I ended up at a gasthaus called the Lamplight in Bitburg. And there I would meet a wonderful "fraulein" … a young, unmarried German woman. I shall very affectionately refer to her as, "Heidi." With blond hair and blue eyes, she certainly caught my eye and so I asked her to dance. She knew very little English and was from Duisburg, a town just north of Dusseldorf, about a two and half hour drive north from Bitburg. She happened to be passing through with her sister and her sister's boyfriend. I couldn't speak German but we did our best to communicate with our hands and drawing on napkins … somehow my German improved as the pilseners went down. Anyway, I got her phone number and a girlfriend relationship was to begin and lasted throughout my two-year tour. Shortly afterward, my roommate Terry met Heidi's friend "Christiana" (whom he'd eventually marry the following year).

And our crew of Lou, Steve, Jeff, Keith, and Bruce would form a party crew of sorts. I even bought a 1966 Volkswagon Beatle for a mere $125. However, the gas pedal was a screwdriver through a cable, the emergency brake was a rock from the Pruem Air Station NCO Club parking lot jammed under a wheel, and the starter didn't work. But parking on a slight incline to roll and "pop" the clutch, and she started just fine (if not on a hill, then Lou would push)!

Back on base, the Non-Commissioned Officers Club (NCO) Club on Bitburg was a hopping place during the '70s disco era. And the East Germans knew it too, especially on Friday or Saturday nights. At least once a month, they would send a few MIG (Mikoyan & Gurevich) fighter jets screaming toward the border, only to turn back at the last minute. But it was enough to trigger radar warnings and scramble our F-15s toward the border. Bitburg had four F-15s on "Zulu" alert. That is, fully armed, 24 hours a day-7 days a week, airborne in 5 minutes. Of course, that triggered our sirens and everyone had to hurry to their duty stations and grab their chemical gear. It was quite a sight to see everyone pile out of the club and dorms at 2 am in a, let's say, not-so-prepared-to–fight condition. I remember the distinct sound of people scrambling in the dorms all pissed off and swearing and struggling to carry their gear, while chasing the unique sound of their steel pot helmets rolling down the stairwells!

During the Cold War, the East German Air Force was a military branch of the National People's Army (Air Forces of the National People's Army). Known as the LSK (Luftstreitkrafte der Nationalen Volksarmee), it had a variety of aircraft provided by the Soviet Union that were the most advanced of its time among Warsaw Pact countries. Its roundel emblem was black, red, and yellow emblazoned with the communist hammer and compass: the hammer representing the workers and the compass representing the intellectuals (the thinkers, skilled professionals, scientists, etc). Its main fighters in the late 1970s were the MIG-21 (known as the "Fishbed") and the MIG-23 (known as the "Flogger"). The West German Air Force, or Luftwaffe's, main fighters in the late 1970s were the Lockheed F-104G Starfighter and the McDonnel-Douglas F-4E Phantom II. Often the German F-104s would perform low-level strafing runs on the base during exercises and really rattle and shake everything and everyone.

MIG-23 (Known as the "Flogger")
(Creative Commons)

By July 1978, I was rapidly learning and working the F-15 egress system. We had a few aircraft losses that year, but its ESCAPAC ejection seat system worked as designed. As such, I would earn a "Save" on an aircraft that had mechanical problems and went down near Daun, West Germany. A "Save" is basically an acknowledgement of a successful ejection of a crewmember after recent maintenance was performed by a maintainer and team member (egress maintenance is a demand-response 2-man team). Ironically, the pilot was from Chicopee, Massachusetts near my home town of Springfield ... how very gratifying that was! Unfortunately, we would have a few more crashes in 1978 and '79. All had successful escapes except for one who was unable to attempt to eject and crashed into a mountain. That recovery was a gruesome process as we pieced together what was left of the egress and canopy systems. The base gym where he worked-out was named in his honor ... the Mike Mark Memorial Field House. During this time, I was promoted to Airman First Class, six months below-the-zone (BTZ)! BTZ is a competitive process for early promotion for exceptional Airman who stand out from their peers and perform duties at a level above their current rank. Despite my early challenges and setbacks in the Air Force, maybe I finally found my niche in this career field.

By September, I was selected to go on my first temporary duty (TDY) assignment with an egress Staff Sergeant. We were sent to Nea Anghialos, Helenicon Air Force Base, near Volos, Greece for 32 days in support of Commander-in-Chief, United States Air Forces Europe (USAFE), Operational Order named, "Display Determination." We stayed at the small sleepy resort village of Nea Anghialos, which was about eight miles from the base. Our mission was part of a North Atlantic Treaty Organization (NATO) exercise as part of reinforcements to bolster the southern region of NATO and served as an inter-allied training effort. Other exercises in Turkey were also being conducted. Of course this was a great opportunity to showcase the new American F-15 Eagles ... and perhaps persuade Greece to rejoin the NATO military command.

Lockheed F-104G Starfighter (Creative Commons / Cropped)

Greece withdrew from NATO's integrated military structure in 1974 after Turkey invaded the northern portion of Cyprus in response to a military coup. The Greek Cypriot paramilitary was attempting to annex the island to Greece. The war lasted a month and killed over 3,000 people, which ended in a ceasefire. The island was basically split in half and the ceasefire line became the United Nations buffer zone or "Green Line" (Turks in the north and Greeks in the south). Greece was not happy that the United States did not stop the invasion by Turkey, a fellow NATO member. Protests and riots occurred in front of the American embassy in Nicosia, and its ambassador, Rodger Davies, was assassinated. The international community only recognized Cyprus's independence from Great Britain in 1960 and has sought withdrawal of all foreign forces from the island. But such was not the case in 1978 when we were sent there.

Our aircraft maintenance team made the five-hour flight from Germany to Greece on a fully loaded C-130 Hercules cargo plane. As we prepared our flight line section at the Greek Air Base for the arrival of our F-15s, I couldn't help but notice the number of high level Greek military brass and dignitaries that were there. As each jet landed and uniformly parked side by side, the pilots waved and gave their thumbs up at the welcoming party as they shut down their engines and opened their canopies. I thought that this was a pretty impressive sight and thought it was a delight to our hosts and a good start to our stay considering the recent history here. But I couldn't help but notice that some of our hosts were not pleased and seemed to be annoyed and somewhat angered by some of the pilots and maintainers. Perplexed, we later found out that it was very difficult for us to refrain from hand gestures that were deemed offensive despite given cultural briefings … perhaps with not enough emphasis to its importance.

Later at the hotel, we found out that several members of our team did hand-waves and thumbs-up gestures. The five-fingered hand wave to Greeks is called the "Moutza" and is received as calling them an idiot (or an asshole as we know it). This gesture, followed by our thumbs up is like giving them our middle finger. Not to be outdone, all this followed by our "OK" thumb and index finger circle gesture is a sexual insult … kinda like "Go Fuck Yourself" (GFY as we know it)! I'd say all in all, not a great first impression. After a bit of a hearty laugh, we couldn't believe we "shot our self in the foot" so-to-speak. As Americans, do you realize how hard it is NOT to give these gestures? Guess we were in for a difficult start and a bit of a challenge to overcome. Fortunately, our assigned guests liked to drink Amstel beer and eat souvlaki (kind of like a shish-kabob meat on a stick) … we were really good at that too … only to be outdone once again by trying their Greek Ouzo; a 90 proof aperitif that is widely consumed there.

The Greek (Hellenic) Air Force at that time were flying American-made F-104G Starfighter, Northrop F-5 Freedom Fighter, Vought A-7 Corsair II, McDonnel-Douglas F-4 Phantom II, and French made Dassault F1CG fighter aircraft. So it was a real treat for their top General to get a ride in a two seat F-15B! Many of the maintainers were betting their General couldn't handle the G-force of a max climb take-off and would throw-up. To my chagrin, I'm glad he didn't because myself and a crew chief would have to clean up the mess! Meanwhile, the respect level and relations improved and the exercise and social events went well, despite the embarrassing start.

We flew an outstanding record of 138 sorties tasked and 138 sorties flown for a 100% in mission accomplishment! This helped open the door to a new era of military relationship between the U.S. Air Force and Hellenic Air Force.

We also got a couple days off to go visit historic sites. So off to Athens I went with a couple of buddies! I had always wanted to see the Acropolis, a hilltop citadel with the Parthenon temple, and the many ancient Greek ruins which were abundant everywhere throughout the country. We also took a boat cruise to Skiathos Island in the Aegian Sea, best known for its beaches and waterfront clubs. (Greece would return to NATO's military structure in 1980).

Then back in the Volos area, we went to a sheep farm that makes the shaggy flokati rugs. We all bought many rugs and souvenirs during our stay. Getting them back to Bitburg was another story … to better international relations, of course. But, you could only pack so much additional stuff in a C-130 ... but we found a way on an empty F-15 engine stand!

BITBURG AIR BASE, WEST GERMANY, 1979

Upon returning from Greece, I spent the fall and Christmas holidays of 1978 with my German girlfriend at a train station farmhouse in Hohenfels. What a very nice time in the scenic German countryside and then later in a fun city in Duisburg. Time away from base was such a nice reprieve from our constant stressful war-preparedness posture. We liked to party and the German beer was very good! My buddies and I often took tours to places like Verdun, France and Bastogne, Belgium, or into Luxembourg to see war sites and party. Going into 1979, our work-hard play-hard mentality was a tough balance as staying on 12-hour shifts didn't leave much in a 24 hour day … but I did have youth on my side. Being young does have its advantages!

During these years under President Jimmy Carter, we were very much in the "Hollow Force" mode. This characterized our post-Vietnam military forces appearing to be mission-ready, but actually suffered from personnel, equipment, and maintenance shortages and deficiencies in training. It was a budget-cutting process that became a trade-off between readiness and modernization. This was particularly dangerous in West Europe as the USSR, East Germany, and other communist bloc countries were at its Cold War height and the western allies were not faring well. One could easily imagine the communist tanks breaking through the Fulda Gap to overrun Europe … and as such, we were at the front lines: my brother Ronald in the eastern and myself in the western part of West Germany. Meanwhile another fallout from the Vietnam War was that over 3 million people died of execution, disease, and starvation under communist Cambodian leader Pol Pot's reign and the follow-on Cambodian-Vietnamese War. That was a very disconcerting time to my Vietnam veteran supervisors with a very bad taste of how that conflict ended … and of its aftermath. Also, the Panama Canal treaty was signed by a one-vote Senate margin turning over ownership of the canal to Panama. We felt we were losing the Cold War on many fronts.

Cannibalization of parts from one aircraft to another was one method to attempt to stay mission-ready. This was a very stressful maintenance practice. Many times an aircraft would land in good shape, but then maintainers would remove a good part and put it into a broke airplane to make it fly … only to remove it when that plane landed to put it back into the original airplane. Of course, this sometimes involved removing the ejection seat to gain access to the part! This was very time consuming as we doubled maintenance time to make sorties. And then there was much in-fighting when a part was damaged in the process, as well as the challenges of keeping the records straight, for you then could have two broken airplanes!

Compounding this maintenance challenge was not only a shortage of maintainers but also Security Policeman. At the time, the Security Police (SP) consisted of two areas: Law Enforcement and Security. So the concept of augmentees (augies) was used in the Security area. So myself and one other Airman from the shop were selected and trained (Warskill AFSC W81132). Thus, when the MIG fighter jets came screaming toward the border and trigger radar warnings, and our F-15s scrambled toward the border, us auggies would get our Mission Oriented Protective Posture (MOPP) bag, chemical gear bag, and M-16s with real ammo magazines at the armory. Off we went, as the sirens blared while everyone scurried to their duty stations and grabbed their chemical gear. Of course, it was quite a sight to see everyone pile out of the club and dorms at 2 am once again, in a, let's say, not-so-prepared-to-fight condition, once again. Even a few auggies were reluctant to report. I remember one guy, telling the Sargent, "You can't send me out there, cuz Jack Daniels says, so," as he blew a breath on to the Sergeant. Ole Sarge said, "You'll sober up real quick out where I'm sending your ass!" Usually that meant out on a hilltop by the F-15 bomb dump or ammo bunker areas … in January or February!

That being said, I remember those cold 12 & 13 hour shifts out there alone in the cold. A truck might stop by after six hours and toss a "sack nasty" (food bag) over the fence yelling, "Bon appetite!" It would be quite cold too. I remember trying to stay warm tucked up inside a Light-All unit, which we weren't suppose to do because of a carbon monoxide poisoning hazard. But, its doors were open and I had a good view, and I would make fence-line rounds every 20 minutes or so. Aside from our Cold War enemies of Soviets and East Germans, another great fear was of being probed or attacked by the Red Army Faction terror group.

The Red Army Faction, also known as the Red Brigades or Baeder-Meinhof Gang was a West German far-left militant organization founded in 1970. The group had its origins in the 1960s among the radical elements of the German university protest movement. They believed that America was an imperialist power and the West German government was a fascist holdover of the Nazi years. Their activity peaked in late 1977, which led to a national crisis and series of terror attacks that became known as the "German Autumn." U.S. soldiers and airmen stationed in Germany were repeatedly terrorist targets in the 1970s through the mid-1980s. Although the death toll was fewer than 10 in a series of a bombings spread over a decade, scores were wounded. Such was the environment and some of the threats we experienced … as aircraft mechanics with M-16s on a hilltop guarding a munitions storage area.

After the collapse of the communist government in East Germany in 1989 - '90, and the end of the Cold War, it was later discovered that the Red Army Faction had been given training, shelter, and supplies by the Stasi, the secret police of the former communist regime. Greatly weakened by the demise of communism throughout Eastern Europe, the group announced an end to its terrorist campaign in 1992.

(Creative Commons)

In the midst of this, we stayed busy on details. In the military, especially lower ranking personnel, were frequently tasked with additional duties or taskings. One such duty was as a flight line driver delivering aircraft specialist and mechanics to various aircraft. With 75 F-15s at Bitburg at various locations, it was crazy responding to radio calls and coordinating with one other truck driver to pick up and dispatch technicians, their tool boxes, special tools, and large volume technical orders (TOs) or manuals. Our call signs were Green 1 and 2. The constant tug of war over who had priority was frustrating with the Job Control center, but we got good at managing the jolts and re-redirects. Life on the flight line in all weather conditions and MOPP conditions when the sirens sounded, were all part of our "Hollow Force" and Cold War challenges in West Europe. Of course, the endless details didn't end there. General base cleanup and other "volun-told" activities continued. But at night we polished our boots and sipped beer!

One such tasking was helping maintain a static display F-86 Sabre jet on a display pedestal by the base front gate by the Bitburg bowling alley. This was a more enjoyable job since we were working on a real history airplane. We set up maintenance stands, taped-off the canopy, prepared other surfaces, and assisted on its paint job. We were proud to work on this Cold War gem. Conversely, we also helped transition the new F-15C models to Soesterberg Air Base, Holland.

(Creative Commons / Cropped)
Moved From Bitburg Then Refurbished and Installed at Spangdahlem Air Base, Germany 2006

But there were many fun times too, such as Germany's version of Mardis Gras known as "Fasching." Usually this "silly season" is for a full week each February. Many downtown clubs would host costume parties. One day is devoted to the ladies, where they would visit local establishments in masks and they would like to paint people's faces and offer them a drink, for a small fee of course. On another day, they would like to cut men's ties in half with scissors. Then there was the Wittlich Pig Festival. According to legend, the town was a walled fortress. One night the guard lost the town gate key and used a carrot to secure the latch. But a pig came along, ate the carrot, and the gate swung open and the town was ransacked. The angry townspeople have roasted pigs ever since! The Bernkastel wine festival on the Mosel River was another fun time for a week in early September. The ruins of the old Landshut Castle is the highlight with fireworks and lots of wine to sample ... I remember waking up in the back of an Army deuce-and-a-half truck with several drunk soldiers parked on the bank of the river. Then there was the Bitburg Annual Summer Happening (BASH) on the air base, which was a great base-wide party each year during the fourth of July weekend. Lots of Bitburger beer and bratwursts were shared with the town locals who were allowed on base as guests.

By September of 1979, I was promoted to E-4 Senior Airman and was selected as Airman of the Quarter for the base, the 36th Tactical Fighter Wing. Heidi began going to a university in Duisburg and we still spent weekends together in a loving relationship with several trips alone together peaking with a great time in Paris, France. For several months, I had also been working weeknights at the NCO Club as part of a nightly clean-up crew. I made enough money to buy a nice stereo system and fund my forays to see her and later have a good time with my buddies.

By late September I took a 10-day trip with my buddies to Austria, Switzerland, Liechtenstein, Italy, and then to the Oktoberfest in Munich, Germany. That was a fantastic time! But one of our last stops was to the Dachau Concentration Camp where 41,500 were killed by the Nazis. After such a great time it was also a hard dose of historical reality of the Holocaust just some 34 years ago (at that time) … the genocide of six million Jews across Nazi-occupied Europe. But it was also a solid reminder of how we got here as part of this Cold War life.

As we entered the end of 1979, my party crew and I were receiving permanent change of station (PCS) orders and we were all getting "short" (time's running out here). The farewells would soon come. One by one, we would assemble at the "White Swan" bus stop near our beloved F-86 Sabre jet. There we would have final toasts of Berentzen Apfelkorn Schnapse and tearful waves. Growing from 18 to 20 years olds, we all had shared a very important part of our teenage life together. These two years were one big non-stop event-filled times growing from boys to men. Now it was on to our next chapters in life. But I still had a month of my Bitburg assignment left as I entered 1980, and I would be one of the last of our group to leave.

During this time, I was selected as Airman of the Year, 1979 for the 36th Equipment Maintenance Squadron! Its grand prize was an incentive flight in a two-seater F-15B! It involved some altitude chamber, escape system, and physiological training at nearby Wiesbaden Air Base and several briefings before the actual flight. I was fitted with a flight suit and helmet and even wore the rank of Captain with its silver bars on my shoulders. I was teamed-up with Captain "Tank" Payne of the 53rd Tactical Fighter Squadron … and off to the flight line we went! There she was, aircraft tail number 76-0124. How different it felt to be arriving at an airplane without a tool box in my hand. As we approached the airplane, a crew chief greeted us and escorted us up into the cockpits. Instead of kneeling in the ejection seat performing maintenance, I would be actually sitting in the seat getting strapped-in by a crew chief. From a maintainer to a flyer, this day would be very special indeed, as we taxied out of our USAFE (United States Air Forces Europe) TAB-VEE shelter (Theatre Air Base Vulnerability Evaluation Exercise).

On this cloudy overcast morning, 11 January 1980, we took off, not in a max climb as I had hoped, but as a 3-ship team with two other F-15As. This would be an actual one-hour training mission against other F-15s from a sister fighter squadron from Bitburg.

In coordination, "Tank" would let me have control of the jet for a few brief moments. He'd tell me to move the stick left for an easy barrel spin left, level off, then stick right for easy 360 degree roll right. It was so easy to maneuver this airplane. Our two other team jets gave us space and let us have fun for a while. But as we approached our battle space air box area, it was time for the pro to let loose and dogfight it out for a while. "Tank" took over as we engaged the "enemy" jets, pulling high Gs, rolling left and right, as the gun cameras were firing "shots." I felt the flight suit inflate and deflate to the ever-changing G-forces. It was the most intense amusement park roller coaster ride that I had ever experienced! Hitting up to 5 Gs, I got a bit disoriented and dizzy, but loving every minute of it. The other two jets would also engage the opposing force and its dog fights would ensue. After a good while "in the box," it was time to "knock off" and return to base. At altitude I was able to take a few photos with my camera of one of our team Eagles (76-0032). Once we landed, taxied in and parked, I enjoyed watching the crew chiefs doing the hand signals to the pilot during taxi, engine run up, then shut down. As "Tank" opened the canopy, what a joy it was to be on the seated receiving end in the cockpit as the crew chiefs installed the safety pins into the ejection seat and assisted us exiting the aircraft as they began their basic post-flight inspection and checks. "Tank" would give the crew chiefs an overview of any aircraft maintenance discrepancies as they reviewed the "781" maintenance log.

The aircrew bus was there to pick us up and bring us to the fighter squadron building for debriefings. We then turned in our helmets and flight suits and gear and went to another room with the other aircrew teams and opposing force teams to watch the gun camera footage. We would cheer or boo at each other depending who got shot down or shot at and learn from the various maneuvers each made. I believe we got shot down once but shot two down during our engagements. Although this experience would occur well before the "Top Gun" movie came out in 1986, it sure felt like I was part of a Hollywood production this day.

(US National Archives)

67

In December, I received orders to Homestead Air Force Base in very Southern Florida near Miami. I would be working on F-4D Phantom II fighter jets of the 31st Tactical Fighter Wing. I thought wow, that would be so great to be on a beach there in February! My items were then picked up and shipped off to Florida. With less than a week to go, my final moments with Heidi were also winding down. Thoughts of marriage were there … maybe start a new life together in Florida, much like Rhiannon and I attempted to do to start a new life after high school. But we weren't quite there and still very young. The break-up episode with Rhi was still fairly emotionally fresh for me from just over two years ago. It was best to let things be for now. Heidi came to see me off at the bus stop that cold morning. With a tear in my eye, I was off to Rhein-Main to see my brother Ronald, then depart from there back to the USA.

Before leaving Bitburg, even after a great incentive flight, I wanted to reflect on the Cold War aircraft losses during my time at Bitburg and of 1Lt Mike Mark (6 Jul 78).

- 17 April 1978: F-15A, *75-0059*, of the 525th TFS, 36th TFW, USAF, crashed into the North Sea off Cromer, Norfolk, UK. Pilot ejected with minor injuries.

- 15 June 1978: F-15A, *76-0047*, of the 53rd TFS, 36th TFW, USAF, crashed into the North Sea. Pilot ejected safely.

- 6 July 1978: F-15A, *76-0053*, of the 53rd TFS, 36th TFW, USAF, crashed near Ahlhorn, West Germany. Pilot was killed.

- 19 December 1978: F-15A, *75-0063*, of the 525th TFS, 36th TFW, USAF, crashed near Ahlhorn, West Germany. Pilot ejected with minor injuries.

- 28 December 1978: F-15A, *75-0064*, of the 22nd TFS, 36th TFW, USAF, crashed near Daun, West Germany. Pilot ejected safely.

- 3 June 1979: F-15A, *76-0035*, of the 53rd TFS, 36th TFW, USAF, crashed on landing at Bitburg Air Base, West Germany. Pilot ejected safely.

- Shortly after my incentive flight and departure from West Germany, three more Bitburg Eagles would go down in 1980 … I believe I fared well on the January timing of my flight:

- 4 March 1980: F-15A, *75-0070*, of the 22nd TFS, 36 TFW, USAF crashed near Baden-Baden, West Germany. Dog fight training mission. Pilot did not eject and was killed.

- 6 March 1980: F-15A, *75-0082*, of the 22 TFS, 36 TFW, USAF crashed near Bitburg Air Base, at Castle Hamm, West Germany. Pilot killed.

- 25 July 1980: F-15A, *76-0013*, of the 525, 36 TFW, USAF, crashed near Spangdahlem, West Germany. Pilot ejected.

(F-15 Accident Database, Aviation Safety Network, December 10, 2021)

Meanwhile, my incentive flight aircraft 76-0124 would fly a full career. It ended up at RAF Lakenheath, England performing as an aircraft battle damage repair (ABDR) training airframe in February of 2000. And although no longer flyable, it is still in use and listed as "instructional" status as of September 2021.

(eurodemobbed.org.uk, December 10, 2021)

PLATTSBURGH AIR FORCE BASE NEW YORK, 1980

As it turned out, my orders to sunny south Florida were cancelled and I was diverted to Plattsburgh Air Force Base in very upstate New York, near the Canadian border. Besides the winter weather change, I'd be going from a fighter base to a bomber base. From an F-4D Phantom II fighter assignment to FB-111A Aardvark fighter-bombers. Welcome to the 380th Bombardment Wing (Medium)!

Part of the Cold War posturing between the U.S. and Cuba (and its Soviet influence) was dealing with people fleeing communist regimes. One such episode was the Mariel Boatlift crisis. Between April and October 1980 there was a massive emigration of 125,000 Cubans in about 1700 boats from the Port of Mariel near Havana, Cuba, to Miami and Key West, Florida. Although the refugee processing centers were largely handled at Eglin Air Force Base up near the Florida panhandle, I can't help but imagine that I would have been detailed from Homestead to help build tent cities and assist processing as was the case for many others. So probably a lucky assignment diversion for me after all ... and my Bitburg household goods sent to Homestead would eventually be sent to Plattsburgh. By this time, the Soviet Union had invaded Afghanistan and proxy wars would expand.

As I got to Plattsburgh Air Force Base on this very cold February day, I was assigned to the 380th Field Maintenance Squadron egress shop. On the west shore of Lake Champlain, New York and 20 miles south of the Canadian border, this area felt much colder than my Massachusetts upbringing. During this time, there was an Air Force wide crack-down on drug use, thus explained my diversion from Homestead. Apparently, the manning shortage was due to a few shop members getting busted for drugs.

Plattsburgh was in the Strategic Air Command (SAC) and largely dealt with nuclear weapons in its arsenal. Strict adherence to procedures at all levels were highly enforced, especially if you were on the Personnel Reliability Program (PRP) with aircraft maintenance duties tied to such. Drug use could not be a part of that. I was to maintain 30 FB-111A capsule escape systems and two T-37A Tweet trainer aircraft egress systems. This heightened Cold War nuclear weapons posturing was also prompted by the Soviet Union's invasion of Afghanistan. Thus, we constantly moved, towed, and positioned aircraft parking patterns as it was also believed Soviet satellites may have been in overhead orbit (possibly a Zenit series version). Broke or not, the aircraft were out of the hangers looking like they were poised for war.

The base also had KC-135A Stratotanker refueling aircraft. Once the Soviet satellite had presumably passed, we resumed our real maintenance posture … but the hollow force maintenance parts shuffle was still a factor. That posturing was one mode that served as a deterrence against Soviet aggression. One of my details as an airman was to report for duty during heavy snowfalls and drive a tractor with a plow to clear the parking lots, often during the wee hours in the very cold morning.

Meanwhile, the Winter Olympics were taking place at Lake Placid about an hour's drive away from Plattsburgh. And what a time it was! Eric Heiden won big on gold medals during speed skating competition and became the first person to win all five speed skating events at one Winter Games. But our eyes were all on the U.S. men's ice hockey team. We all watched each game on the dorm's "day room" TV. Although the gold medal game was won over Finland, it was the 4-3 upset win over the Soviet Union prior to this that was the real "Miracle on Ice." The Soviet professional team had previously won four consecutive Olympic gold medals. It was the least expected thriller and much needed boost of our national pride. It was also a huge ideological win and part of the Cold War's silent battle.

(Creative Commons)

We all celebrated immensely as this victory was an enormous morale booster for our country as we were lagging behind the Soviet Union on the world stage. If you were alive at that time, this was a colossal moment! The impact of that hockey team's patriotic win planted the underdog mentality in my mind as I watched it unfold before my very eyes. For these college kids, this team had a very strong desire … winning against all odds! As we watched the gold medal team climb the ladder to board the plane at Plattsburgh Air Force Base, we waved and cheered and we all felt a very deep sense of pride … and that maybe we had a chance of turning this Cold War into a winning direction. But in the final Gold medal count it was still the Soviet Union that had 10 medals, East Germany 9, and USA 6. Following Plattsburgh State University's hockey team winning their championships in 1978 and '79, then Olympic Gold of Team USA in 1980, it was fitting being in New York. The NHL's New York Islander's would win the first of 4 Stanley Cups that year as well. It was an exciting time to be in New York, nonetheless.

These changes of fortune gave us hope. But these were short lived as the Iranian hostage crisis was already in its third month. When the pro-American leader, the Shah of Iran Mohammad Reza Pahlavi was toppled by an Islamic Regime, he went to the U.S. for cancer treatment. The Iranian revolution had begun with its new leader Ayatolla Khomeini who was very upset with the American intervention. Thus, 52 American diplomats were taken hostage from the U.S. embassy in Tehran by college students. In the backdrop to all this, was that there had been a coup in 1953 that brought the Shah to power who turned out to be a dictator himself. But he was anti-communist and pro-western and was generous with his oil reserves to America and Britain. The daily countdown of time the hostages were held added pressure to the U.S. government to act. And so they did, on 24 April 1980.

Desperate at the slow pace of negotiations and diplomacy and upcoming presidential elections, President Carter launched Operation "Eagle Claw," and sent an elite rescue team to the embassy compound in Tehran. But a sandstorm happened to occur at a staging area called "Desert One" when the operation was underway. This caused several RH-53 Sea Stallion helicopters to malfunction diminishing the number of helicopters needed for the mission, and the mission was aborted. Then tragedy struck when a helicopter rotor blade made contact with an EC-130 Hercules cargo plane and both aircraft exploded killing 8 serviceman (5 airman on the EC-130 and 3 marines on the helicopter). The failed operation and follow-on humiliation was yet another setback in the context of the Cold War, much to the delight of the Soviet Union … and the daily countdown of time the hostages held was a slow steady drip of helplessness to the American psyche. As military members, we were heartbroken and demoralized and felt somehow we were stuck in a stalemate as the diplomatic stand-off would continue throughout the summer and fall. As a tribute, I would often try to drink eight beers in their honor and do an Eagle Claw "pincher crush" of each empty can … a tradition I still perform to this day (albeit not quite always 8 beers)! At the time, Eagle Claw was my Citizens Band (CB) name (handle) because I often used Eagle Claw brand name fishing hooks and lures.

Meanwhile, during the summer of '80, I had a small beer crew that I'd sometime chum with and sometimes meet at several of the area Lake Champlain beaches. Especially during the summer where it was like "Spring Break" for the Canadians. It was also time for the summer Olympics to be held in Moscow, Russia. But in response to the Soviet invasion of Afghanistan the U.S. put numerous sanctions and embargoes on them and led a boycott of the games with 66 other nations. Saddened for the athletes who could not participate, it became another cost to the Cold War sacrifices that many had paid. But of course, it would be the USSR and East Germany with winning the most medals again.

By September, I was promoted to E-4 Non Commissioned Officer, Sergeant, or affectionately known as "Buck" Sergeant, the lowest Sergeant rank. Now in a supervisor grade, I was put in charge of a night shift with one airman. It was good duty and my work hours were steady and often quiet. So I started going to college at Chapman University to work on my basic core courses. The old base side of Plattsburgh had kept its old buildings and parade field intact and that's where I'd attend classes. This area served the Union troops during the Civil War and military units during the Spanish-American War. It also had a nice marina on the lake but I'd often go fishing for brook trout in area streams during the day. About twice a month I'd make the 4-hour drive home to Springfield, Massachusetts. The drives were gorgeous down the Adirondack Mountains on the New York side or sometimes I'd go across the lake by ferry and down the Vermont side.

Being home again was so different. I had experienced so much during the two and a half years that I had been gone. Basic training, tech school, all the Bitburg involvement and the silent Cold War battles of ideologies that I had underwent … I was now the outsider looking back. A few of my friends also went into the military. But most stayed in their hometown areas, worked, raised families, and settled into their routines. It was nice to visit old bars and local "haunts" and go down memory lane. My high school sweetheart had two kids now, an old-timer friend was murdered, and drugs had taken the lives of a few others. Time puts things into perspective. It was time for me to let go and resume my life. By this time, Iraq had invaded Iran and that would start their eight-year war … but the hostage crisis day-count would continue nonetheless.

Heidi and I had kept in touch and were still together. She came out to New York to visit me. She flew in from West Germany and I picked her up in Montreal, Canada. We visited my grandmother and tourist sites in Quebec, met my friends in Plattsburgh, and my family in Springfield. It was a great time. Marriage thoughts were popping up again. She also expressed she was feeling negative peer pressure at the university for having an American boyfriend because of the ongoing developments in Europe. Meanwhile, I was now working on nuclear bombers and Europe was feeling the effects of the Soviets deploying their SS-20 Saber missiles in the western part of the Soviet Union. NATO was poised to respond and the "Euro-missile crisis" would begin. NATO put the Soviets on notice to come to a negotiated solution or it would deploy Pershing II and Ground Launched Cruise Missiles by December 1983.

In addition, the U.S. proposed production of the W70 version of the "neutron bomb," so it was hard not to talk about this development as protests increased in Europe. That uproar over missiles in 1978 and 1979 pressured President Carter to delay, but not cancel, the program. The neutron bomb was basically intended to replace tactical battlefield nuclear weapons by killing people with neutron radiation and minimize destruction of buildings and other collateral damage. It was focused on Soviet tank crews and not linger long. But with the backdrop of President Reagan electing to produce the "neutron bomb" in 1981, but keep them in storage, it had caused even more fervor in Europe. But the changeover in policy and direction by these two presidents would set the tone for the rest of the 1980s and beyond. For those of us who had lived in Cold War Europe, this was very real. As such, Heidi and I let our relationship stay as it was … enough love to keep us together, but some Cold War cracks in our relationship were beginning to appear. She returned home and resumed school in the universities … where the protests festered and grew.

APPOINTMENT TO
NCO STATUS

380th BOMBARDMENT WING (M)

PLATTSBURGH AIR FORCE BASE, NEW YORK

PLATTSBURGH AIR FORCE BASE
NEW YORK, 1981

Meanwhile, those Cold War realities factored into the November elections that resulted in Ronald Reagan's big victory over Jimmy Carter. As we had entered 1981, the remaining hostages were released from Iran just a few hours after President Reagan delivered his inaugural address ending the hostages 444 days in captivity … and began hope for brighter days ahead for America. But the President was shot in the chest in March by a deranged drifter and in May, Pope John Paul II was shot by a Turkish assassin. Both would survive and recover. These two events would add an additional chill in the context of the Cold War.

But working the '111 in the winter was brutal outside. The wind chill was often in the sub-zeros. I remember trying to safety-wire (secure-locking) shielded mild detonating cords (SMDC) on an explosive panel on the upper edge behind the pilot's cockpit hatch. It contained a self-righting flotation bag in case of an upside-down water escape. A thin .20 wire was used to secure the explosive connector in an "S" fashion. Multiple twists with bare fingers would go numb very quickly even if your teammate was holding a heater over your hands. Well at least blood would freeze if you poked yourself … and it did! Also in cold weather, the cockpit hatch lifter (counterpoise) went flat due to low pressure. Sometimes all that was needed was a little bit of heat blown in to the cockpit to get the lifter to extend to open the hatch. If not, the counterpoise needed to be serviced with nitrogen or had to be replaced. Often they would be over-serviced in the winter to compensate for the cold … but then the pressure difference would catch up in the spring as it got warm and the items would become over-pressurized creating leaks or blown pneumatic seals, requiring unit replacement. But it was winter, and as such was the call I received to service or replace a hatch counterpoise. If unable to service, the aircraft would have to be taken off of alert status, which meant de-arming the aircraft then arming another aircraft to replace that one. That time consuming process meant America had one less potent arrow in its quiver should an attack occur. Yeah, this was real and we felt real pressure. So maintenance techs would become heroes or villains real quickly if you couldn't save the day. Luckily, we were heroes that day.

Trying to perform maintenance on an aircraft on nuclear alert was another experience just to gain access to the aircraft. On a cold winter day of course, we got another counterpoise service call. Upon arrival to the "Christmas Tree" security entrance, we parked our vehicle to begin the security process. At Plattsburgh there were nine aircraft on nuclear alert at an area near the end of the runway. They were angle-parked like "Christmas Tree" branches. They were "cocked" and ready for take-off at a moment's notice. Each carried Short Range Attack Missiles or SRAMs. SAC alert was serious business. That area consisted of the "Mole Hole" or aircrew response facility that had corrugated steel tunnels protruding from it that was located near the alert ramp or "Christmas tree" where the aircraft were parked. During an alert scramble, the crew would scramble down the tunnel to their awaiting vehicle and rapidly transit to their planes. Once engines were started, the aircraft would quickly join in an "Elephant Walk" to the runway behind each other, and take-off in a short interval manner. Rapid take-offs of nuclear armed aircraft were of the essence to respond to nuclear attack.

In SAC, there was the "No Lone Zone" or two-man concept to prevent nuclear tampering. We had mandatory training under the Air Force Nuclear Surety program where either person could detect an incorrect or unauthorized procedure and prevent or deter the other person from that procedure. As such, a "Demand-Response" was established. As an egress technician, we were already performing demand-response as a routine practice as we often worked with explosives anyway. But there was no room for failure and strict adherence was demanded. In this case, my Technical Sergeant and I were able to service the counterpoise … and were heroes once again!

Through all these practices and processes, maintenance was continuous to safely put planes in the air and bombs on target. As such our units were competitive during a SAC bombing and navigation competitions called "Giant Voice" at Barksdale Air Force Base, Louisiana.

Our FB-111s from the 529th Bomb Squadron won "Best Bomber Squadron" and our KC-135A Stratotankers from the 380th Air Refueling Squadron won "Best Tanker Squadron" titles for the 45th Air Division as "Best Tactical Squadron(s)" of the Year for 1980 and taking the coveted General Curtis E. LeMay Bombing Trophy. Such was the process at Plattsburgh and similarly so at other SAC FB-111, B-52, KC-135, and Air Force missile bases. We also had an outstanding performance during an Operational Readiness Inspection (ORI) that determines the readiness of SAC units to accomplish their wartime mission.

Despite the successes of 1980, there were reminders of the cost. The FB-111 had a terrain following radar used for low-level attack flying just above tree level ... sometimes too close. In October one of our aircraft (68-0268) crashed off the coast of Maine killing the pilot, Major Thomas Mullin and navigator Captain Gary Davis. The reality of our mission really sinks in during moments like this. Not every situation allows for rapid use of the escape system. We were all greatly saddened and mourned their loss ... and for egress techs, wondering 'what if' the system could have been activated? We'll never know, but we prepare for the unknown nonetheless. It's about our egress motto ... "Last chance for life."

There were only two FB-111 bases. Aside from Plattsburgh, New York there was Pease Air Force Base in Portsmouth, New Hampshire. However in early 1981, Pease would also lose a '111 near Portsmouth (68-0263). This time, the crew did manage to safely eject. Ironically, the pilot Captain Peter Carellas was from my hometown of Springfield, Massachusetts. This greatly raised our spirits after the October loss. Our egress shops were small, but our community was tight. Despite the loss of aircraft, it is the grief of lives lost ... but also in the salvation of lives saved. Both are Cold War realities that are close to home.

Meanwhile, back at Plattsburgh, there was one man I surely admired. He was our 380th Bomb Wing Vice Commander, Colonel John A. Dramesi. He had recently signed a picture of his hand-made "Freedom Flag" with a personal note to recently released Iran hostage Lieutenant Colonel David M. Roeder. Roeder was also a decorated Air Force veteran who flew some of the first B-52 missions over Vietnam in 1965. The caption on the picture from Colonel Dramesi read, "Let us continue to do as we are expected to do. And to be the men we are expected to be. What is expected is to be expected. What must be endured will be endured." This was an inspiring moment for me and well covered in our base paper, "The Champlainer," and local newspapers. But Dramesi's story is amazing in itself. During his 59th bombing mission flying his Republic F-105 Thunderchief, Dramesi was shot down, but ejected from, his crippled aircraft over North Vietnam.

Upon his parachute landing, he twisted his knee and got into a gun battle with North Vietnamese soldiers and was shot in his right leg before being captured. Thus began his legendary journey as a Prisoner of War (POW) in Vietnam. He would be at two camps, known as "Hanoi Hilton" then "The Zoo," for six years (2 April 1967 to 4 March 1973). He escaped twice and had plans for a third escape. He paid dearly with continuous beatings, starvation, torture, and even sleep deprivation for over 38 days … and still declined propaganda efforts at recordings or letters for his enemy captors. He created an American flag with scraps of cloth that he and fellow prisoners would salute to keep their faith and spirits alive. When he was released as part of Operation "Homecoming" in March 1973 at Clark Air Base in the Philippines, he displayed his "Freedom Flag" out the bus window where the press photographers made it a big story. Colonel Dramesi later presented that flag to President Richard Nixon at the White House.

After presenting the signed picture of his hand-made "Freedom Flag" with a personal note to Lieutenant Colonel Roeder in 1981, Dramesi would go on to become the Wing Commander of the other FB-111 base, at the 509th Bomb Wing at Pease AFB, New Hampshire from June to December 1981. Ironically, I would see him briefly once again, as I was sent on temporary duty to the Pease egress shop for a week in October during a manning shortage. He retired shortly thereafter in 1982.

Colonel Dramesi wrote his autobiography in a book titled, "Code of Honor" in 1975. It highlighted his POW story but drove home the importance of conduct during captivity. During my training in the 1970s and 1980s, the Code of Conduct was always there in our training, study guides, and board questions. It was really drilled into us and many POWs were heroes because they led by example … and we were expected to hold the same standard. Unlike the Geneva Convention, which is an international legal guide, the Code is a moral guide. Thoughts of this did pop into my head when we were out on guard posts and wondering what would happen if we were captured by the enemy. Such was one of my many memories while guarding that F-15 bomb dump or during "bug-out" exercises in West Germany in '79. In addition to security police augmentee duty, there was also a base operability and survivability detail during and after a base attack exercise. Teams were assembled to perform Aircraft Battle Damage Repair (ABDR) and evaluate the non-flyable aircraft and their hardened shelters that housed them. They also had to identify Unexploded Ordinance (UXO) locations all while attempting to deny the enemy any use of our assets … then hopefully still have a timely departure to avoid being killed or captured by the Soviet or East German special forces (or "Spetsnaz" teams). It's amazing what goes through your mind during these exercises.

The latest version of the Code of The U.S. Fighting Force is a Department of Defense directive that still has six articles with minor changes from previous versions:

ARTICLE I: I am an American fighting in the forces which guard my country and our way of life. I am prepared to give my life in their defense

ARTICLE II: I will never surrender of my own free will. If in command, I will never surrender the members of my command while they still have the means to resist

ARTICLE III: If I am captured I will continue to resist by all means available. I will make every effort to escape and aid others to escape. I will accept neither parole nor special favors from the enemy

ARTICLE IV: If I become a prisoner of War, I will keep faith with my fellow prisoners. I will give no information or take part in any action which might be harmful to my comrades. If I am senior, I will take command. If not, I will obey the lawful orders of those appointed over me and will back them up in every way

ARTICLE V: When questioned, should I become a prisoner of war, I am required to give name, rank, service number and date of birth. I will evade answering further questions to the utmost of my ability. I will make no oral or written statements disloyal to my country and its allies or harmful to their cause

ARTICLE VI: I will never forget that I am an American, fighting for freedom, responsible for my actions, and dedicated to the principles which made my country free. I will trust in my God and in the United States of America

(archives.gov/federal-register/codification/executive-order/10631.html / 31 December 2021)

It was during this time that I was promoted to E-5 Staff Sergeant, first cycle, June 1981. As such, the Code was part of our military education process. I remember that promotion notification day well, as General of the Army Omar Bradley had recently died. One of my favorite World War II heroes, he served as a reminder of the many great leaders in our history that had continued to serve us well, till their very end, during my Cold War life.

Plattsburgh Air Force Base continued to perform very well scoring an "Outstanding" rating during the "Global Shield '81" exercise. This was truly an amazing effort to witness as our FB-111s joined B-52 bombers, and KC-135 tankers as massive take-offs within 10 minutes from over 70 bases. It was a spectacular surprise launch of planes responding to a mock nuclear attack. Although unarmed, the short interval take-offs of our SAC aircraft made for a thunderous event. As maintainers, we always got "a front row seat!"

By July, Heidi had returned for another visit. We went camping and fishing and made our rounds in Springfield. Our love was still there but somehow we knew we were drifting apart in other ways that were rather ideological. It was apparent that her university in Germany was giving her greater angst among the socialists. With Reagan as the U.S. President, the European missile protests were increasing in Europe and my first enlistment was winding down. I had some decisions to make. But the Air Force had a Base of Preference (BOP) incentive program at the time and I applied for a return to Europe to Camp New Amsterdam, Soesterburg Air Base in Holland (F-15C base near Bitburg) … or a few California bases. I had enough of real cold weather living. But if I didn't get any of my choices would I get out and not reenlist? We were sitting on the fence once again.

Meanwhile, as the European universities were heating up with protests, the Soviets were spreading their influence in Central and South America. We too were getting educated and very "clear-eyed" on the ideological Cold War that was going head-to-head. In September of '81 while I was TDY to Pease, base members assembled at the base theatre for a "Soviet Awareness" Program briefing … and what a show of realism it would be.

After the National Anthem was played and a reading of the Constitution and other American liberties were proclaimed, the program transitioned to Britain's Winston Churchill's famous "Iron Curtain" speech in 1946 at Westminster College in Fulton, Missouri. It condemned the Soviet Union's policies in Europe and of an "Iron Curtain" descending upon Europe. Aside from the Berlin Wall, he was also referring to an inner German border wall, an 858 mile long wall that ran from the Baltic Sea to Czechoslovakia. His speech is regarded as one of the opening statements announcing the beginning of the Cold War. But the memorable highlight was the transition to patriotic Russian music and a Soviet flag and a big man dressed as a Soviet General marching on to the stage. He commenced to lecture us about the Communist Manifesto summarizing the theories of German philosophers Karl Marx and Friedrich Engels, which became a very influential political document. The "General" went on and raved about the history of class struggles and how our capitalist society would eventually be replaced by socialism and he called for forcible overthrow of all existing social conditions and that this is a call for communist revolution around the world. After he was done lecturing us, we booed and loudly jeered our rejection at him as he marched away to fading Russian patriotic music and Soviet flag backdrop. When the American flag was raised everyone cheered as the base commander came forward to remind us of our mission and steadfastness. It was definitely a very motivating program. In contrast to the Communist Manifesto was our American Constitution Preamble's opening line, "We the people ..." We fully knew who the enemy was and what was at stake for our country, and the world.

As a Senior Airman, I attended the required Air Force Professional Military Education (PME) course at the time which was the NCO Orientation course (PME I) at Bitburg. Then as a "Buck" Sergeant afterward I attended the NCO Supervisor course (PME II) at Plattsburgh. By October of '81, I was proficient as an FB-111 egress technician and earned the Strategic Air Command (SAC) Master Technician Award (earn a 7-skill level and have no failed Quality Assurance Evaluations). I also had received orders to Beale Air Force Base in Northern California. Decision time to reenlist or separate was finally upon me.

Nr. 000032

SOVIET AWARENESS

PROGRAM

1200-1600, 9 Sep 81
Base Theater

NAME *Hamel David L*

SIGNATURE *David J Hamel*

Authorized *[signature]*

JOHN A. BICKNELL, Major, USAF

This pass must be presented with your
ID Card for entrance.

BEALE AIR FORCE BASE, CALIFORNIA, 1982

When the assignment notification came, I had to reenlist to accept it. The report date was to be in late November. It was a very short notice as a position at that base had just become vacant. I reasoned that I got the California assignment I had wanted, but it also put me further away from Heidi. I would at least have some stability for several years with a fresh start. Now it came back to whether Heidi would be a part of that process. I was warming up to that thought, but would she? We'd been together, more or less, nearly four years. After a brief visit home to Springfield, I was off on a cross-country drive in my 1977 Toyota Corolla SR-5, 4-speed, and a new journey was to begin! I greatly enjoyed my first cross-country drive across the USA on Interstate-40 and visited and saw all the sites I could see along the way including the Grand Canyon in Arizona.

As I arrived in the small town of West Linda-Olivehurst, I made the turn toward Beale and it would be another nine miles across flat lands and rice fields before arriving at the base gate in the middle of nowhere. Once I was cleared, I drove through about another four miles of tall wheat-looking grassy plains around the far end of a runway that eventually led to the aircraft side of the base. There I could excitedly see the SR-71 Blackbird hangars and several U-2 Dragon Lady aircraft parked in their areas (known as ramps or aprons).

As my sponsor welcomed me, he informed me that the situation in the egress shop had changed drastically since I departed Plattsburgh. A few members had been busted for drug use and our manpower dropped by four in a 12-man shop. Of the remaining 8, three were sent off to temporary duty locations around the world supporting real world missions. That left 5 personnel: the shop chief to run management and UCMJ actions (Uniformed Code of Military Justice) on the busted four, two to work day shift (12 hour shifts) and two to run night shift (12 hour shifts). With a mandatory two-man team concept in play, that meant one maintenance team for each shift. I quickly sensed that I was about to enter a much higher paced Cold War operations tempo (Optempo) than I had expected.

After signing-in to the 9th Field Maintenance Squadron, I drove across another four miles to what was known as the "cantonment" or residential section of the base. I was assigned a one-bed room in the squadron dorms, unpacked, and was immediately scheduled for escape system training on the SR-71. Known as the Blackbird, the Lockheed SR-71 is a long-range, high altitude reconnaissance aircraft capable of going Mach 3+ (Mach is the speed of sound) at altitudes of over 80,000 feet. During the Cold War, this plane could fly higher and faster than any other. It was designed in secrecy in the 1950s and holds the records for highest altitude in horizontal flight and fastest speed for a non-rocket powered aircraft. It was designed to capture time-sensitive intelligence in denied airspace during a time before satellites and drones began being fully used. It was able to venture into enemy territory without being detected or shot down. The sinister looking aircraft is quite a sight to see. I always marveled just being around it.

I immediately attended and completed the U-2 and SR-71 egress systems courses in early December. But just as I completed this training, the egress shop received a special request from the Edward F. Beale Museum to assist in demilitarizing a Martin EB-57B Canberra they had recently acquired from the Burlington, Vermont Air National Guard (tail number 52-1526). This aircraft was being retired from the inventory and they were looking for egress personnel to deactivate and de-arm its two-seat egress system. As it turned out, the Canberra had a very similar ESCAPAC ejection system to that of the F-15 A and B. The maintenance squadron Chief Master Sergeant (E-9) was an egress technician who had worked those systems years ago and needed an experienced specialist to work with him (as the egress 2-person concept still applied). In their search, I, the new guy, who just left FB-111s and T-37s, found myself on an old Cold War bomber as my first maintenance job at Beale … not an SR-71 or U-2, but an EB-57 … because of my F-15A experience! What a baffling way to start this assignment!

(Creative Commons)

Although the Martin EB-57B Canberra was designed as a tactical bomber and served as "Night Intruders" in Vietnam in 1965, it did serve in SAC as a high altitude reconnaissance platform as an RB-57D. That mission would be replaced by the U-2 and SR-71. By 1973, several of the Canberras would be converted to an electronic counter-measure role as EB-57s. The canopy system was very bulky, but the seat item explosives were very similar to other systems. It took us about a week to remove and demilitarize, and tag and turn-in explosive items and components. I really enjoyed working on this vintage Cold War airplane. But it was time for me get busy on the Blackbirds. I then immediately went to work on the flight line, in the phased inspection hangar, and in the egress shop, and quickly focused my training experience on the SR-71. There would be no break through the Christmas holidays.

Into 1982, there was no break in work-load either, but there were milestones in history to be a part of. On 19 January I got to support the launch and watch the completion of the 1000th flight of a trainer SR-71B, tail number 17956. As it roared by, I could see the 1000th sortie in huge white letters on its rudder and underside. This particular aircraft featured a higher raised rear canopy behind the pilot's canopy and distinctive stability fins underneath the engines. I would get to know this aircraft very well during my time at Beale as I was often called upon to search for dropped tools or objects in the rear cockpit, which was a very deep and cavernous area. But, one could be an instant hero if dangled upside down to retrieve such items … and prevent a lengthy canopy and seat removal job. I was that guy! … a true FOD-Fighter (Foreign Object Damage). But this would be only the beginning. In only two months, I was put on Red X orders (to clear and sign off aircraft maintenance forms) and about to go on my first temporary duty directly supporting operational missions.

In February, off I went to Royal Air Force (RAF) Base Mildenhall in Suffolk, England. I flew on a KC-135Q, a re-fueler aircraft designed to support the Blackbird with a special type of jet propellant fuel known as JP-7. After a very long flight, I arrived at the base, which is located about 74 miles northeast of London. Known as Detachment 4 (Det 4) of the 9th Strategic Reconnaissance Wing, the base also hosted U-2 operations of Det 4. During my time there, I participated in a SAC Operational Deployment called "Giant Reach." During that time, there were two SR-71As (tail #s 17980 and 17964). Their taskings were stand-off surveillance missions in generally three regions over international waters such as in the Barents Sea (the Kola Peninsula outside of Murmansk areas), the Baltic Sea, and off the coast of West Germany. Largely, it was monitoring the Soviet Navy's Northern Fleet activity along the Norwegian fiord region and eyeing their land-based mobile missile sites and nuclear submarine bases. Most missions were photo-reconnaissance and helped verify Soviet adherence to the Strategic Arms Limitation Treaty known as SALT I. The agreement between the United States and the Soviet Union was a partial freeze on the number of offensive nuclear weapons each side could have. (Many of these classified missions were later de-classified and became known as "Baltic Express").

In the backdrop to these missions during these years, especially after the Soviet Union's invasion of Afghanistan in 1979, it appeared the Russians were still on the march. Thus, the fear of Soviet intervention into Poland was very real. Much news was coming from this area as these actions did occur in Hungary in 1956 and Czechoslovakia in 1968. To pre-empt such an intervention, the communist leader in Poland (Wojciech Jaruzelski) imposed martial law in December of 1981.

His paramilitary police dispersed demonstrators, imposed curfews, levied censorship on all media, wire-tapped phones, and caused increased food shortages. This crackdown suppressed protests and deepened the economic crisis. Despite the news propaganda at the time from the Soviet news agencies Tass and Pravda, we knew things were dire in Poland and the grip of communism in the Eastern Bloc was still very firm. (These actions would eventually lead to huge protests by the trade unions by the end of 1982).

(Shutterstock)

Mildenhall was a cozy area among rolling farms with Shetland Ponies. But the Bob Hope Recreation Center near the Galaxy Club on base had a tradition since the 1950s called "Hog Call," where local British farm girls came to dance and party. These women who were eager to meet an airman would come in groups from nearby towns such as Cambridge and Norwich. They would get together and organize their own bus-loads and have someone sign them in to the club. The lack of base fences and gates made it easier at the time (pre 9-11 of course.) The building was a bit dilapidated at the time, but it had its own charm. I remember it as quite an entertaining event to meet the ladies … many of whom found their "beau" (and not make their scheduled return time back on to the busses)!

Outside the gate there was an old English tavern called the "Bird in Hand." Here we'd play darts and sip pints of Abbott Ale. The maintenance guys and I made a few wine-tasting raids at Cambridge and local area pubs such as in Newmarket or Mildenhall town itself. Personally, I loved the visit to the Bury Saint Edmunds ruins of the Abbey where the Magna Carter was signed in 1215. That document established that the king and his government were not above the law and placed limits on royal authority, and that the people can have lawful dissent. Of course, much later in history this document would have strong influence on the United States during the American Revolution and development of its Constitution and Bill of Rights. It definitely still had strong resonance for the Western European nations against the totalitarianism governments in Cold War Warsaw Pact nations in East Europe. But most enjoyable was when Heidi came over from Germany. We went to London and toured the city and areas around the Thames River. It was almost like old times.

As my time was winding down in England, I wanted to see her one last time. We had a brief break in SR-71 missions and I was able to take leave for a couple days and go to Dusseldorf, West Germany. Despite our very enjoyable time in England, we sensed that time was quickly running out for us. She was now in a left-leaning university environment, and being with an American was now not popular at all, especially in the backdrop of the Euro-missile crisis. Protests were also going on in England at RAF Greenham Common and bases elsewhere. We met at an outdoor cafe and I dressed as European as I could with nothing flashy so that I could somewhat blend in with the locals. But I could tell she was not comfortable with me being there … and I was quickly beginning to feel the same way too. In this very Cold War environment, I was wondering if the Soviet foreign intelligence and domestic security agency (KGB), East German Security Service (Stasi), or American agents from the Air Force Office of Special Investigations (OSI) or Army Criminal Investigation Division (CID) had tracked me from England expecting to catch any suspicious activity or a trap. Did the British Security Service (MI5) track her from West Germany to RAF Mildenhall … and back? My situational awareness had the hair raising on my arms. We were probably closely being observed. Although nothing came from this, we both knew then that our new life directions were at a crossroads yet again. We would close out our four-year Cold War love story here … back in West Germany, where it all began. As much as I loved her, and she loved me, and yet so grateful for this relationship, it was with a very heavy heart, knowing that it was time for us to let go. I returned to Mildenhall greatly saddened and heart-broke that realities of the times had caught up with us. I resumed supporting a few more SR-71 missions and my replacement from Beale came in. I finished-up my tour at Mildenhall at the beginning of April of 1982.

Meanwhile, the Brits were gearing up for their battle with Argentina over the British territories of South Georgia and South Sandwich Islands as they were headed into the Falklands War (Malvinas Islands) in the South Atlantic. Their undeclared war started just after I had left, and lasted 10 weeks. I was unaware if there were any SR-71 mission planning or involvement at the time towards that effort, as our mission focus was still generally in the Baltic region and the U.S. was technically neutral during the Falklands conflict. Near the southern tip of Argentina, tanker refueling support would have been very difficult also. Either way, maintenance personnel were seldom knowledgeable of any of the mission details. We just launched and recovered aircraft as required … but it would have not been surprising to us if it did occur.

Once I returned to "Mother Beale," (a return "home" from deployments or from detachments) in California, I didn't really have time to unpack. I was able to attend a few base functions in April but then I was quickly sent to Patrick Air Force Base near Cocoa Beach, Florida in May and June of 1982. I was there to support U-2 missions as part of a newly formed Operating Location "Olympic Fire" (OL-OF). Our focus was keeping an eye on the Atlantic and Caribbean areas of activity. As the Cold War raged in Europe, it had also had been spreading into America's southern hemisphere. Having the Space Shuttle launches at nearby Cape Canaveral surely may have attracted attention also.

Much like the "containment" policies since the end of World War II, most Latin America states were poised the same way under the Rio Treaty of 1947 ... basically, an attack against one was an attack against them all. It was a doctrine of defense in the hemisphere. Despite facing the common communist threat, many rivalries started to unravel from the one agreement that bound them together. With Cuba being the regional bad actor since its revolution in the late '50s leading to the rise of Fidel Castro, it began to inspire insurgencies and copy-cat rebellions. It peaked with the Cuban Missile Crisis of 1962. Despite the Soviet withdrawal of its medium range SS-4 and intermediate range SS-5 missiles at that time from Cuba, it did not leave them undeterred (and it was a U-2 that produced evidence of their presence there). But it was enough to plant the seeds of Marxist movements and propagate subversion and ideological clashes of capitalism with undemocratic regional regimes. In the peripheral Cold War strategy, Soviet proxy nations were fomenting from within geopolitically. Although not aligned into a federation of sorts as the East Bloc countries of Europe, Cuba was still the central player, and other proxies would emerge.

The Soviets had quietly resumed arms shipments being funneled into Latin America with the hope of replacing governments with communist pro-soviet regimes much like Cuba. As such, the U.S. backed and funded right wing rebel groups such as the Contras who were opposing the Marxist Sandinista Junta government of Nicaragua (that also had a large Cuban military presence). Honduras would become a staging area for much of the support operations (and covert activity for the CIA). These actions and patterns of activity would bleed over into neighboring countries such as Guatemala's and El Salvador's civil wars throughout the early and mid-1980s. Drug trafficking and its associated cartels would also factor in these operations. Such was the backdrop and tone of the regional turmoil that was occurring ... and worthy of monitoring.

While there, we had our U-2 airplane on display for the base's "Fly In '82" airshow on Patrick. I also had a chance to see the Space Shuttle Columbia on Pad 39A at Cape Canaveral at the JFK Space Center prior to its launch on 27 June. I also watched WESTAR V Delta rocket lift-off carrying a communications satellite. The 1980s were an exciting time for space activity and I never tired of tracking their flights. This was good duty with a lot of time on Cocoa Beach.

(Shutterstock)

Once I returned to Beale Air Force Base I received T-38A Talon egress certification training. The base had 15 of these aircraft that were flown for qualification of Blackbird pilots. But after training, it was time for airshow support … and part of that was having a T-38 on display, and there I was. At Beale in July, we hosted a large one with almost 30,000 people viewing the events. It was the largest crowd ever at that time at Beale. Airshows are a great time. But if you are a host, it is a lot of work with set-up, security, and cleanup. The prime attraction that year were the Navy's "Blue Angels" that flew their A-4 Sky Hawks and put on a great show. But airshows in July are also very hot. However, just a week later I loaded and boarded a KC-135Q and flew to Offutt Air Force Base in Nebraska for its airshow. There, I supported an SR-71 and U-2C model. It was a huge show with 175,000 people. But my highlight was recovering and retiring the last active Air Force C model U-2, tail #56-6701, (Gary Powers shoot-down era-type), where it's now on display at the Strategic Air Command Museum in Ashland, Nebraska.

But one of our maintainers was injured when a TEB transport container lid blew off in the cargo storage area in the hangar. TEB (Triethylborane), is a highly explosive chemical fuel igniter for the SR-71. Its JP-7 fuel is flash resistant and needs TEB to ignite it in the engines. Being outside the building, several of us heard a loud echo 'boom,' then several 'ker-tinks' as several container fasteners struck the inner door, then a metal cover hitting the floor. Apparently, a container pressurization malfunction occurred during container servicing. The individual received forehead and a facial lacerations that definitely could have killed him … and lucky for us too, no one else was hurt.

The flurry of summer activity continued two weeks later with a return to OL-OF for 10 days to conduct a phased inspection on the U-2. We performed our mission and returned to Beale. But again, two weeks later, I boarded a "Q" and was off to the Toronto International Airshow in Canada to support the SR-71. After a 5-day stint there, I returned in time for intense base preparation for an upcoming SAC Inspector General inspection in early October. I was finally able to catch my breath for a 4-week reprieve up through the Thanksgiving holiday before I was again sent to Patrick in early December for another 65 days with the U-2. Closing 1982 became a blur rolling into 1983.

Spending Christmas in Florida was a treat. I was single so it enabled the married guys in our egress shop to be home with their families. My time with Heidi probably closed at the right time. I could have never known the heavy Cold War OpTempo (operations tempo) that I was about to walk into this year once I left England. But here I was, soaking up the sun, working out in the gym, doing runs on the beach, and enjoying some of the local night life with the guys.

I remember a U-2 launch during a misty, low-ceiling morning. We sat in our maintenance truck awaiting a C-130 Hercules to take-off before we could proceed. Just as the C-130 rolled down the runway, a flock of pelicans came out of nowhere and 5 or 6 of them got chopped up by the propeller blades. Undeterred, the ole 'Herc lumbered away and up she went without a hitch! But now we had these large one winged birds flapping away on the runway, a bloody mess, with bird parts everywhere. The U-2 is an air breather and could easily ingest these birds or the center wheel could roll over one and trip the airplane as it balances on that center wheel. The van driver got the clearance and a few of our maintenance folks were farm guys. They were "chomping-at- the-bit" to break a few necks and toss the ole birds aside, while a few of us others had brooms to sweep away the rest of the mess. In minimal time, the aircraft still made its scheduled take-off.

On a separate U-2 recovery, the plane landed with a fuel transfer problem. It landed with one wing heavy. Each wing had pogos or training-wheel type supports that were installed into each wing to taxi on. Unable to transfer fuel to balance the wings, a few of us laid on the left wing and hugged it tight as we could. The weight was enough to install the pogo into the right wing. Three of our bodies were enough to balance the wings, and enabled the aircraft to slowly proceed down the taxi-way to its parking spot in front of the hangar. I also had to use the North American Rockwell OV-10A Bronco egress shop at Patrick to store our ejection seat and rocket during maintenance. They took care of us and brought us out on a few of their launches. Certainly not as impressive as a U-2, but I gained an appreciation of its Cold War mission and history. Such is life in maintenance!

(Creative Commons / Cropped)

(US National Archives)

BEALE AIR FORCE BASE, CALIFORNIA, 1983

By late February 1983, it was back to "Mother Beale" once again. This time I jumped into the new TR-1 Spyplane (Tactical Reconnaissance) world as we accepted the new two-seater TR-1B in March. Since my arrival at Beale in 1981, the new TR-1 Spyplanes were arriving. The airframe, engine, and escape systems were the same but with an upgrade to the horizontal tail section. This new platform was ideally designed for its mission for European operations. The new 17th Reconnaissance Wing at RAF Alconbury in England would be the recipient of these aircraft and the U-2R at Det 4 Mildenhall would return home to Beale. The Warsaw Pact was increasing their buildup of tanks, troops, and missiles in East Europe with the help of the usual cloudy weather and better camouflage techniques. The TR-1 had the newer radar and sensors to track that tactical threat versus the U-2. In the backdrop to this activity was President Reagan's "Evil Empire" speech in March, as the Soviet Union was the "focus of evil in the modern world."

By April, I went out to celebrate my 23rd birthday with a couple of guys from work at a disco in Marysville, California near Beale. There, I met a beautiful woman who caught my eye and I asked her to dance. Ironically, she was there with two of her friends. Out of love, respect, and privacy again I shall affectionately refer to her as "Angela." We danced some more, talked, and I got her phone number. She was also in the Air Force as an E-4 Sergeant and worked on Beale in the Personnel office. She too was busy working these deployments and personnel moves. Thus, we shared some commonality and a relationship quickly started. She had a 4-year old son and he and I bonded well from the start. Being single and never having kids myself, I thought a child would complicate this relationship. But "Mikey" made it so easy for me to like him and she was a good mother with disciplining him. I was excited about this relationship. It had been 13 months since Heidi and I had parted ways, and I had been gone so much during this time supporting Blackbird missions. Would I be ready for another Cold War relationship? Well, at least Angela was an American airman serving on the same base and supporting the same missions.

During this time, I was selected as the 9th Field Maintenance Squadron Maintenance NCO of the Month for April. It was really nice to be recognized for my work performance. But by May it was time for me to pack up and go again for another 65 day stint … and ironically it was Angela who was processing the assignments in Personnel! This time it was to the East Asia theatre of operations to support U-2R missions at Osan Air Base in South Korea. Detachment 2 of the 9th Strategic Reconnaissance Wing had two aircraft there. And I would meet and get to spend time with the famed unit mascot, "Oscar," the Black Cat. I'm not sure where he got his name, but I assume it's probably associated with the local Oscar drink, a fruity-type wine. Anyway, the unit flew "Olympic Game" mission tracks along the demilitarized zone (DMZ). The country was still a very dangerous place as the 1950-1953 war never ended but was still in a truce. We would stay very busy with our daily flying and maintenance demand.

Osan Air Base is 40 miles south of Seoul and 10 miles east of Suwon. At the time, it was home to the 51st Tactical Fighter Wing that flew McDonnell-Douglas F-4D/E Phantom IIs and North American OV-10As. As a detachment (Det 2) we flew nearly daily with one aircraft up and the other used as a "spare" or back-up, or in maintenance. We spent a lot of time in our maintenance truck to support launches and often had to "wing-walk" the aircraft as it navigated along the F-4 parking revetments (defensive blast walls) as it taxied to the runway. It was often a tight clearance with its 104.8 foot wingspan. We were also allowed "morale" calls once a week for 5- minutes on the Secure Telephone Network (STN), which had to go through the Beale operator then connect to your local phone line. It often had echoes.

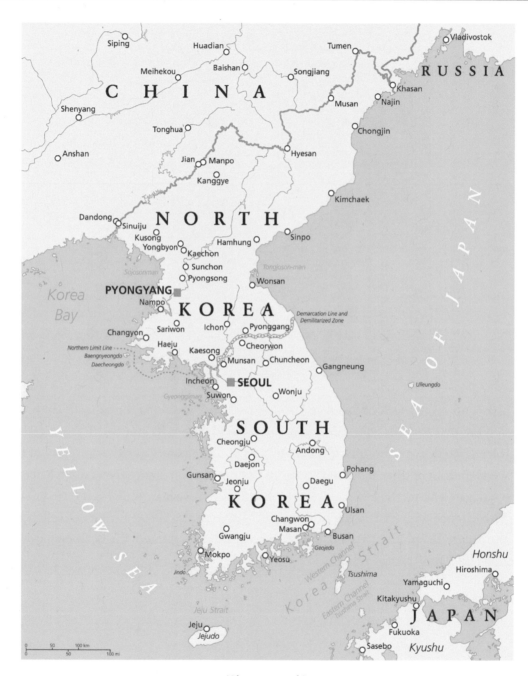

(Shutterstock)

A time or two I had to bring an ejection seat drogue chute to nearby Republic of Korea (ROK) Suwon Air Base, about 17 miles north. It had a chute re-pack capability at that time that we didn't have. Suwon also had newly arrived Fairchild A-10As increasing to 26 attack jets. It was a very busy time and one could feel that the war was still on and not over. The atmosphere and posture of the military and civilians, although quite friendly, reminded us of such. But, we often made our way downtown to Songton City to frequent the bars, restaurants and shops as the exchange rate with the Korean Won currency was very good.

In the context of the Cold War, North and South Korea were formed as part of the World War II partitions, much like North and South Vietnam after the Japanese were defeated and East and West Germany after the Nazis were defeated. Geography and political differences of the separated sides made it difficult to reunify each. In each case, agreements for elections never materialized and in each case the opposing side were communist regimes. For Korea, China and the Soviet Union were its northern neighbors and would not accept a reunified free Korea. Thus, a proxy war turned into a full-fledged war when the north invaded the south in June of 1950. That three-year war went back and forth up and down the peninsula until a United Nations truce was signed at the 38th parallel where it still stands today at Panmunjom.

During my time there, I would buy teddy bears and stuffed animals for Mikey and gifts for Angela during my nightly forays with the guys before hitting the bars. I preferred the OB Beer (Oriental Brewery) versus the Crown Beer. Others would gain their fill of Oscar, the fruity rice wine. Peach was favored most, or Makgeoli (Makkoli) a raw rice wine. Of course the real knock-out was Soju, a Korean rice wine that had an unusual punch. One could be laughing or crying profusely depending on its individual effects. Often, a chalky vitamin mix was added to Soju known as Backus-D. We also ate good meals with a variety of kimchee or cabbage and vegetables … or nibbled on speckled bird eggs.

A friend of mine Gene and I decided to take a bus ride to see the General Douglas McArthur Park and Monument at Incheon. The Battle of Inchon was a 4-day fight beginning with amphibious landings in September of 1950, which led to the recapture of Seoul two weeks later. It was a decisive victory and resulted in a reversal of the enemy advance on the peninsula. While there, two bus loads of young Korean students arrived as part of a history class. I was immediately singled out as an American dressed in shorts (which most Korean men did not wear at that time) and a bright yellow shirt … I was obviously not Korean. My friend being Japanese-American was a bit more subdued and was laughing as he took pictures and the kids swarmed around and kept thanking me, "Kamsahamnida, Miguk!" (Thank-you, America!). It was quite overwhelming shaking hands with these kids, but I could visibly see the schoolteacher was pleased at the episode. Fortunately, I did know how to say, "You are welcome" in Korean, "Cheonmaneyo!" … and so I became somewhat of a hero that day. We all took pictures as Gene and I watched them re-board the busses, and we all waved good-byes. What a heart-warming day to see children learning their history and being so appreciative of their freedoms. Kudos to their teacher and a key reason why South Korea has been so successful today.

I also went with a Catholic Church group while there to the local Shin-Myong Korean children's orphanage providing food, clothing, and entertainment. We cooked hot dogs and had an Easter egg hunt with the kids. In July, the base held a base-wide MASH Bash as part of its 4th of July celebration and later celebration of the Korean War Armistice.

The famous MASH series was having its grand finale during its "Goodbye, Farewell, and Amen" movie concluding 11 seasons. What an awesome time to be in Korea to celebrate the show's setting. Everyone dressed in their favorite MASH clothes. I was also able to make a visit to the DMZ. Upon entering the United Nations Command (UNC) Joint Security Area (JSA) in Panmunjom, in uniform, I had to sign a Visitors Declaration (UNC1 Form 12 EK Nov 81). It acknowledged that we were entering a hostile area, and had information and instructions before given a visitors badge. On it stated that the information provided "will be used as emergency data in case of hostile actions while personnel are in the JSA and to relieve the UNC and associated governments of responsibility." Well, I guess that gets as real as it gets.

We went to see the tree stump where the "Korean Axe-Murder" incident almost restarted the war in 1976. Two American soldiers were sent to trim a poplar tree near a crossing bridge where they were bludgeoned by North Korean soldiers. We were able to go right up the tree area. It was a gnawing feeling being there and a reminder that I was still standing at the last real war front of the Cold War. As my time at Osan was winding down and our missions remained vigilant, we did a group photo as SAC's "Pearl in the Orient."

The last go-out downtown was called a "Brown Bean," unlike a first cat-walk, called a "Green Bean." To get "beaned" is probably synonymous with getting "hammered, slammed, or pounded" … well, Soju does do that. But it was time to return to "Mother Beale." It was so good to be "home." In August, I was able to briefly meet Brigadier General (retired) Charles "Chuck" Yeager after an SR-71 orientation flight at Beale. Another great American hero of mine, he was a double ace in World War II and set a speed record in 1953. Once back from Korea, Angela and I got to spend time together despite the work demands.

We enjoyed the rest of the summer with Mikey and we'd often go camping and fishing in Northern California. The Sierra Nevada mountain range and Lassen Volcanic areas were beautiful. We even took a very long cross-country ride in my '77 Toyota to see the sites along the way and meet her parents in Tennessee. We also made stops in Massachusetts to see my family and attended a wedding and graduations … yeah, it looked like we were doing very well together and Mikey couldn't be happier. The ride back was just as fun.

I had also resumed my church activities at St Joseph's Church in Marysville. As such, I was inducted into the Knights of Columbus, a Catholic fraternal charity organization. At Council #1869, I advanced through the first two orders of Charity and Unity, then third degree Fraternity (full member) by the end of 1983. During this time, I collected "tootsie roll" donations for the handicapped and was selected as Knight of the Month for April 1983 (and later November 1985).

Meanwhile, we continued to do SR-71 missions from Beale. Its credibly long reach, with much tanker support, was quite awesome. Cuba, Nicaragua, Central America, and the Caribbean area continued increasing with communist activity. That meant more time in the egress aircraft launch support truck and supporting this year's frequent very long-leg missions. Also, Exercise "Solid Shield '83" was an annual event where 47,000 U.S. service personnel conducted maneuvers in the Cuba and Central America areas in April and May. During that time, the SR-71 would show presence in those airspace areas as well.

Another area of interest, some 100 miles north of Venezuela was the island nation of Grenada. A coup toppled the government and a request for help to the U.S. came from the Organization of Eastern Caribbean States to help restore the government. Of concern was the 600 American medical students on the island. Fears of them being used as hostages, like the Iran hostage crisis, loomed also. The SR-71 and U-2 soon reconned the island area. The U.S. then launched a military intervention in late October and expelled the Cuban military presence there. Known as Operation "Urgent Fury," the operation lasted four days.

I continued doing great work and was selected as the 9th Field Maintenance Squadron Maintenance NCO of the Month for October, 1983. I was quite proud of that honor for the second time that year. In our egress workshop, we'd often remove parts to facilitate other maintenance (FOM) or prepare items to turn in as due in from maintenance (DIFM) and store them as needed. We had plenty of simulators and special tools for the job too. Always on call, we used "beepers" on and off duty all the time. By November I'd do another airshow support mission with the SR-71 and the U-2 at March Air Force Base in Southern California. But I would stay on to complete a four week course at the 15th Air Force NCO Leadership School at March and would graduate in December, just in time for Christmas. Thus, I would close out 1983.

BEALE AIR FORCE BASE, CALIFORNIA, 1984 - 1985

My Knights of Columbus civic activity also deeply involved many fund-raisers leading up to the construction of the first Columbian Retirement Home for the elderly that year. I then helped restore a nearby historic Gold Rush period cemetery, and was later inducted into the Patriotic fourth degree order (Sir Knight), during the summer of 1984 (Santa Maria Assembly #1959). I was elected and served three one-year terms as Worthy Recorder (Recording Secretary). I was also a "Blessed Brick" project crewmember that removed and cleaned 1,000 bricks from a 130-year old church yard wall and sold the bricks as a fundraiser at $2 each. I continued to assist several fund-raisers and raffles for a Pomona, California council for a second Columbian Retirement Home (that was later built in 1996). I had a great time with this group of guys who had fun and got things done. I was quite proud to be a big part of the "Surge with Service" program that led to two Star Council Awards for 1984 (and 1985). Angela and Mikey would also join in many of the church activities.

Meanwhile, I spent a lot of time on the flight line. California had hot dry days but they were quite tolerable for me. With low dew points, I enjoyed being out there. The variety of work made it fun on the T-38, U-2C and CT models, TR-1A and B models, and the SR-71A and B models. It also required constant diligence using the Technical Orders (TOs) or maintenance manuals. Watching aircraft take-off and land, or fly-bys of other visiting aircraft, were just as entertaining. I was proud to be a part of a big military team. But sometimes things go awry and crashes occur. Such was the case, when a Marine A-6E Intruder (#152585 from VMA AW-121) did what seemed to be a fly-by, but then had some kind of malfunction and crashed in a fireball at the end of the runway. The Grumman A-6 Intruder is a two-seat, side-by-side, attack jet largely designed for navy aircraft carriers.

When you hear a 'poom-poom,' then an explosion on the flight line, maintainers know something good, and very bad, has just happened … then you hope to see silk (parachutes) before the emergency sirens head out. Fortunately, the pilot and navigator did eject safely. These were sounds one really does not want to hear and a reminder of the inherent dangers of egress … but a reminder that the ejection seats do work when you need it, even though we knew that A-6 had a different escape system (Martin-Baker). But we continued to confidently and safely work the escape systems on our T-38 Talon uninterrupted in a hangar as this happened, as the aircraft and grassy fields were ablaze and the firefighters went to work. When in the midst of working with explosives, it is best to ignore distractions no matter how obvious they may be and remain focused on the job.

(Creative Commons)

A week later, while in the SR-71 phase hangar replacing egress explosive components, the hangar shook with another familiar explosion. Though too far to hear a 'poom,' my mind raced for a hopeful successful exit to whatever it was that had crashed. This time it happened to be a TR-1A (#1072). Its tail section had somehow come off during take-off and the pilot had to eject. At such a low altitude, he got maybe one swing out of his chute before he hit the ground, but at least he got out safely. Once the crash site was secure and the grass fire was out, I was selected to go out on a crash recovery to assist the Explosives Ordinance Disposal (EOD) unit in identifying and securing any live egress explosives components. I remember being real sweaty covered in burnt black grass ash on that very hot July day.

(US National Archives)

But then we lost a U-2 at Beale on May 21 and another U-2 at Osan that October. In each case, the spyplane's tail section blew off (tailpipe failures) … but each pilot ejected safely. By this time the U-2/TR-1 fleets were grounded. After 7 weeks, tailpipe adaptor clamps were modified and the problem was solved before resuming flights. But we in the egress shop remained proud of our maintenance with no loss of life and remained true to our motto … "Last Chance for Life," yet again. During this downtime, I was sent to Williams Air Force Base near Chandler, Arizona for 5 days for T-38 egress system certification for the single-motion seat modification. Up to this point the pilot had to rotate a handle and squeeze a trigger to initiate ejection, losing valuable life-saving time. The seat was modified to fire on a "single-motion" handle lift. I enjoyed seeing the Casa Grande National Monument and area saguaro cactus. There were ruins of Ancestral Sonoran Desert People, which I found quite fascinating.

Once back at home, Angela, Mikey and I resumed our travel and camping forays to the coast at Point Reyes National Seashore and seeing the Redwoods in the Avenue of the Giants. By October, Beale hosted another airshow with some 25,000 visitors. But by Thanksgiving, word of reported SR-71 flights over Nicaragua were becoming more known sparking a "Peace Vigil" outside the base's main gate. Although peaceful, their signs were promoting U.S. non-intervention in Central America. Nonetheless, operations would continue. In December, I was on a team on a SAC Operational Deployment, "Busy Relay" supporting a U-2 aircraft switch-out to and from Korea. There were nice stops at Hickam Air Force Base, Hawaii and a follow-on to Anderson Air Force Base, Guam. Other Busy Relays were for SR-71 switch-outs at Det 4 Mildenhall. But these were my first times travelling in the Pacific theatre. Not bad places to be in December, and we were able to get some beach time too at Tarague Beach in Yigo near Anderson. We got back to Beale in time for Christmas too!

By the beginning of 1985, Angela decided to separate from the Air Force and try civilian life working in nearby Marysville. By this time, we were in a serious relationship and got engaged. We moved into a mobile home park in the nearby town of Linda after selling my mobile home that was on base. For me, the OpTempo continued but it was nice to get a nightly break away from it by being off base. Also, our shop manning was back up to where it should be which also lessened the strain as the new guys were now beginning to become proficient on the various escape systems. By March of 1985, the size of the TR-1 fleet at RAF Alconbury had also grown to six aircraft and Beale was supporting Blackbird operations worldwide. But that was the Cold War life that we were now accustomed too. Meanwhile in May, President Reagan made an 8-minute stop at a German war cemetery in Bitburg, West Germany as part of the 40th anniversary of the end World War II in Europe. It became controversial as it contained some Waffen SS graves. But he did a follow-on visit to Bergen-Belson concentration camp up near the North Sea where some 50,000 were buried in mass graves. Such were the continued sensitivities of the times after being stationed there.

Despite an impressive "save" rate with my various egress shops and co-workers over the years, the job remained inherently dangerous. One guy I worked with lost two fingers while removing a T-38 seat when they got wedged in the seat rails as the seat was being raised. But the biggest shocker in June was when I got a call from a dear friend, Judy. I hadn't heard from her in a few years. She and her husband David Andrade and I were great friends while stationed at Plattsburgh as David and I were working the FB-111s there. They were both from New England so we shared the same hometown area interests. They were now at Shaw Air Force Base in South Carolina. He was still an egress technician but working on RF-4Cs. The McDonnell-Douglas F-4 Phantom IIs were a widely used Cold War fighter-bomber workhorse.

She calmly asked me to sit down before she announced what she had to say. As I did, I caught my breath and stared at Angela who was in the living room. We both immediately sensed that something was wrong. Judy then informed me that David had an ejection seat accident and had died. Something went wrong and the seat rocket had fired and catapulted him up high in the air before coming down on the right wing and unto the ground … I was envisioning a very ugly sight. Judy remained calmed and composed as I was quickly tearing up and breathing deep. She still had two young children at home to contend with. In June, I would attend his military funeral in Massachusetts among many other friends and co-workers from our "egress families." This loss really hurt and was a sobering reminder of work hazards of our duty. Between aircraft crashes, accidents, and OpTempo escalations, the Cold War also had quiet costs that became very personal.

Plattsburgh AFB NY 1980-81

(Wikimedia Commons)

Upon returning home, I tried to resume some sort of civilian life enjoyments despite the cost of freedom to attain it. So in mid-June, Angela, Mikey, my sister Lisa, and I embarked on an 11-day drive we called the "California Gold Run '85." It was a wonderful journey making a large loop along the Gold Rush towns in the Sierra Nevada Mountains and tent camping, then going west across to the coast, then a southern drive all down along the scenic ocean coast to the Los Angeles area sites. This included The Missions, Universal Studios, and Mikey's favorite, Disneyland! We then visited with relatives in the same areas before returning home. A bit tiring but a very fun time.

Returning back to Beale, I was able to perform maintenance on an SR-71 ejection seat at the SR-71 simulator. A rarity to do so, it was quite a treat to see it. It is a front cockpit full-scale mock-up of the Blackbird and was primarily a training and procedure trainer. To my understanding only one was ever made. Though there were no live explosive components installed, it did require occasional cleaning or adjustments. I don't quite remember what the call was for … probably a look-see at egress related items such as seat D-ring issues as part of scheduled maintenance and system checkouts.

I do remember being asked if I'd like to go for a ride. Sure enough, I was thrilled to! The simulator tech set me in, put the headsets on, enclosed the cockpit, and gave me instructions for take-off. I focused on the display, pushed the throttles, and attempted a take-off. The actuators and sounds were realistic enough to make it rumble and shake to feel like actual movement of the airplane. Once off, I tried to circle around for a landing but I didn't do well at either, as all kinds of alarms were going off and I knew I was in trouble and crashed. I was reminded I had an ejection seat if all failed, but I certainly did not have time to react. If a real dummy was needed to do a system test, I was the right guy. Flying in an ejection seat and working on one are two very different emotional experiences.

(NASA)

Meanwhile, back on the U-2 ramp I continued to work aircraft and do what we do best. But one October day, a KC-135A Stratotanker was doing "touch-n-go's" (briefly land, no-stop, resume takeoff). Thinking it was one of our "Q" models I didn't think much of it. But this day, I glanced to see the aircraft do a hard left bank before losing sight of it by the U-2 shelters. Seconds later, we all heard a loud explosion as the ground really shook, and a huge fireball erupted as it crashed in a field a mile or so behind us. There would be no 'poom – pooms' as the tanker does not have an ejection system. Apparently, the left outboard engine pod scraped the runway, caught fire, and exploded. All seven crewmembers were killed. It was a KC-135A (#59-1443) from Castle Air Force Base near Atwater-Merced, California, which supported B-52 operations. The KC-135 is a four-engine re-fueler that was the real workhorse for the military, servicing just about everything that flew during the Cold War (illustrated is a similar KC-135A). In memoriam are: Major George T. Nistico Jr, 34, (pilot), Captain James Berkeley Henry, 29, (co-pilot), Technical Sergeant Claude Franklin Arden, 33, (flight refueling instructor), Captain Susan O. Scott, 32, (pilot-trainee), 2nd Lieutenant Kevin Glenn Bryan, 23, (navigator-trainee), 2nd Lieutenant Robbin K. Armon, 28, (co-pilot trainee), Sergeant Desiree Loy, 25, (boom operator-trainee).

(Creative Commons)

By September, I had a promotion notification (line number) for Technical Sergeant (E-6)! That meant I was eligible to attend the SAC Non-Commissioned Officer Academy at March Air Force in Southern California, the same base where I attended the Airman Leadership School. Upon return, it was right back into aircraft maintenance … this time for the SAC Maintenance Standardization and Evaluation Team visit. Basically, a Quality Assurance team comes in from the Major Command (SAC) and evaluates the quality of maintenance and procedures being conducted along with its equipment, programs, and proficiency. But I noticed my airman had placed 5" reflective tape on 3 of the 4 canopy transport carts … they were suppose to be 6." With minutes to spare before the inspection, and to his dismay, I had him place 5" tape on the last cart so they would all look uniform and not draw attention to the disparity. They would either be all wrong or all right. The inspector saw them as all the same and did not notice. After the weeklong inspections, we were rated, "Excellent"… but the lesson of the misfolded handkerchief during my failed basic training inspection was remembered, understood, and utilized!

Back on the home front, we all seemed to be doing ok and some sense of stability was in place for Angela and Mikey despite my long days. I was still able to do some church and civic and volunteer activity and earned a "Knight of the Month" Award for November. I also earned $25 as part of an Air Force suggestion award program for improving technical data guidance on lap belt removal procedures on the U-2 and TR-1.

As 1985 was winding down, the Cold War was still raging on in Europe and Central America. In November, Cuba fired Surface-to-Air (SAM) missiles at an SR-71 during a reconnaissance run. The Blackbird eluded the Soviet made SAMs and had made two sweeps over the Port of Mariel. The flights did confirm that Soviet and Bulgarian ships were transferring war materials to Nicaraguan freighters. Some of these items were tanks, artillery, and planes to be used against U.S. backed Contras, and were far in excess of any defensive needs. The increased presence of Soviet-bloc ships in Cuba as part of "in-direct" shipments from the Soviet Union, marked an escalation of activity in the region.

BEALE AIR FORCE BASE, CALIFORNIA, 1986

After the Christmas holidays, I was off on another short-notice 30-day stint with the U-2 to an undisclosed location in the Caribbean. Bouncing between supporting SR-71 and U-2 flights were real-world mission realities for us at Beale and abroad. The events in our southern hemisphere were viewed as an attack at America's "under belly." Still, we enjoyed ourselves as best we could away from home in the very hot and steamy weather, sometimes getting some beach time and other times sipping some umbrella drinks … with high rum content of course. Many of the guys had a taste for Bacardi 151. Because of its alcohol proof level of 151, we joked we had become "Detachment 151." It seemed the New Year was off to an ok start. (By 2016, the Hamilton, Bermuda based rum company discontinued sale of the product. It was flammable and came with a warning label and a stainless steel flame arrester crimped on to the bottle's neck. Undoubtedly, there were associated safety issues).

But at times, these missions or deployments would come at a cost. The away time and constant life interruptions can have a negative accumulative affect. As such, midway through this deployment I got the call from Angela. She expressed that when I returned that she wanted to leave California … ouch, I was speechless! I had sensed things were not right with her before I had left but I was still in shock. We were together nearly three years and were engaged. But she had a change of heart and wanted to go back east to live with her folks and go to school. With a week left to go on our mission, I was heart-broke and stressing a bit struggling to understand what was happening to us.

The next day, 28 January, our maintenance guys wanted to watch the lift-off of the Space Shuttle Challenger on TV. It was to be the 25th space shuttle mission. As such we all marveled in amazement as she had a wonderful launch from Cape Canaveral, Florida. Seventy-three seconds later, Challenger exploded sending the rocket boosters in different directions killing all seven crew-members. We were among the millions who witnessed the tragic event live as the pieces fell into the ocean. Unrelated, later, we got word that a Beale Airman was arrested for trying to sell SR-71 secrets to an undercover FBI agent posing as a Soviet spy. Just the thought of a traitor amongst us was heartbreaking enough. This was a triple-wammy shocker to me after yesterday's news from Angela ... even the Bacardi couldn't fix this. (Airman First Class Bruce Ott would later be sentenced to 25 years in a Federal prison).

I returned home in early February and tried to understand her position. I still loved her enough to drive her to Tennessee, then I was to fly back to California. It was hard to let her and Mikey go ... and leaving on Valentine's Day made it even tougher. I wished them well and off I went. But then it was like insult-to-injury after a heart-break. A levee break of the Yuba River in Linda-Olivehurst, California areas occurred shortly after we had left. The great floods of Northern California had begun.

Almost ten feet of water would inundate my mobile home and I would lose much more than a relationship. I lived in an area behind the Peach Tree Mall in the town of Linda. My car and almost everything I had owned, much little I did have, was now gone. I would have some significant recovery operations to do. Over 21,000 residents had fled and 43 people were injured when the levee broke with no warning. Beale Air Force Base would also serve as an evacuation center and took in about 4,500 refugees from the affected areas. I stayed at a co-workers house as I was unable to enter the flood zone for another two weeks until the water receded (thank-you, Steve O'Neal!). After doing my time the FEMA (Federal Emergency Management Agency), American Red Cross, and Salvation Army processing lines with the other displaced people, I tried to recover what I could.

During these difficult times I cried and prayed. Then I saw an old sign at a damaged church advertising an upcoming baptism ... I didn't know whether to laugh or cry. Maybe it was a friendly reminder from God. I knew I was really starting over in the midst of this personal baptism ... the sludgy waters flushing my tribulations away. Through all this, I would wallow through the muck and mud, and stench of dead pets, trying to help neighbors, especially the elderly trying to recover, chasing looters away, and stare in disbelief at the various water-line level marks on the trees, buildings, and highway underpasses.

Despite all this, there was a Cold War to fight and the mission continued. Despite the hardships, I pressed on. I knew I wasn't alone in this battle. But there were other hidden costs that come to light that surely rattled my emotional well-being once more. I had a friend in one of the maintenance shops who got into a domestic dispute with his wife in base housing on Beale. She was able to leave the house but two children stayed with him. After a stand-off with security police, Staff Sergeant Mark Trinkkeller shot and killed himself, but the children were unharmed. It was another major heart-breaker that we all didn't need.

Meanwhile, I bought another vehicle and found an apartment and got on as best as I could. After the 150-foot levee breach area was filled and shored up, I walked on top of the one-mile levee stretch gazing at the scar-gap that the flood waters had carved. I began to run the newly filled levee, almost every day it seemed during these "cry-runs." In the following months, as the gouged earth filled in, grass started to grow … and then the flowers came. I increased my mileage and ran other damaged area levees. As the earth slowly healed … I slowly healed.

Back at the egress shop, we kept up with the pace of in-shop and flight line maintenance at Beale. Aside from Beale's T-38s, aircraft rotational and maintenance support of our Detachments became routine. We went wherever needed to meet the mission. For our team, that meant units at Det 1 Okinawa (SR-71s), Det 2 Korea (U-2s), Det 4 RAF Mildenhall (SR-71s), 17th Reconnaissance Wing Alconbury, England (TR-1s), and Operating Location "Olympic Fire" (OLOF which became Det 5) Patrick Air Force, Florida (U-2), as well as all the other "pop-up" missions or operating locations. (There was a Det 3 at RAF Akrotiri, Cypress, (U-2), an island in the Mediterranean Sea, but I did not have an opportunity to directly support that operation during my time at Beale). We were truly a worldwide operation involved with various real world events and keeping a pulse on missions everywhere.

In the greater scope of the Cold War, President Reagan had named Libya, Iran, North Korea, Cuba, and Nicaragua as a "confederation of terrorist states." Several escalations with Libya's leader Muammar Qaddafi had occurred including his "Line of Death" demarcation at the north edge of the Gulf of Sidra and the rest of the Mediterranean Sea. In March, Libya had fired SA-5 missiles at U.S. Navy F-14 Tomcats and missed. But the Navy responded with an A-7E Crusader destroying the SAM site with its missiles. I would later meet that aircrew and F-14 at a Beale Air Show, which complemented the movie "Top Gun" that year.

These incidents and the bombing of a disco in Berlin, Germany prompted a U.S. response, which led to airstrikes in Libya at Benina Airfield and Tripoli. On 14 April 1986, Operation "Eldorado Canyon" began. The force consisted of 18 Air Force F-111Fs tactical strike planes accompanied with 3 EF-111 Raven electronic warfare aircraft (to jam Libyan radars), and 14 Navy A-6Es. All were supported with over 20 KC-135A and KC-10A re-fuelers. On 16 and 17 April, Det 4 provided the post-strike reconnaissance of the targets using both SR-71s. As the attacking force left, it was expected that the Blackbirds could be flying into a hornet's nest of angered Libyan defenses. As such, SAMs were launched at both aircraft without hits. Sadly, an F-111F was lost with both crewmembers during the raid. In memoriam are the pilot Captain Paul F. Lorence, 31 (Missing in Action - MIA), and the weapons system officer Captain Fernando Ribas-Dominici, 33 (body recovered).

Meanwhile, back at "Mother Beale" an immense feeling of pride and accomplishment were shared in the mission's success. (In August of 1987, Det 4 would launch both SR-71s once again against Libya to image Libyan bases and confirm the presence of the newer MIG-29 Fulcrums). Det 4 interactions with Soviet Fighters in the Barents Sea areas also increased with MIG-25 Foxbat aircraft with newer more sophisticated air-to-air missiles firing at the Blackbirds, again unsuccessfully. These were still very hot times. But, the good news was that I was officially promoted on 1 June 1986 and I sewed on Technical Sergeant stripes (E-6)!

Through it all, we still hosted a large airshow at Beale in August with 50,000 people featuring the Air Force F-16 Thunderbirds. A great show it was! But once again as hosts, many of us maintenance personnel were in uniform walking amongst the crowds and keeping an eye on the aircraft. All part of the additional duties for aircraft maintainers.

By late August, I got another short notice selection for a two-week return to "Det 151." And like the last go-round, someone peeled off the Bacardi Rum bottle and really liked the bat on its label. And thus a similar bat appeared on the aircraft's tail … kinda fitting, we thought. As the rum story goes, hundreds of fruit bats were attracted by the sweet smell of the boiling molasses that is used in making rum and were living in the rafters of the distillery. And since these bats pollinate the sugar cane crops and prey on insects that damage the crops, they were viewed as friendly to the rum industry and were allowed to remain. Culturally within the region, they were seen as an image of "good fortune".

However, one night very early in the morning, our Security Police (SPs) saw some lights in the bushes across the runway. I remember the crew chiefs shutting off the light-all unit as our armed security sped towards the area. We dispersed but remained by our maintenance truck and waited as we thought our mission had been compromised. But apparently, some locals were roaming too close and got plenty of attention, but were deemed "not hostile." We resumed our operation shortly afterward. Apparently, the "good fortune" of the bat was indeed with us!

During the summer, I had made a family visit back to home-town Springfield, Massachusetts to do a reset after the Angela break-up and the California floods. It was nice to be home and catch my breath, so-to-speak. But lo-and-behold, I would have a chance encounter at a restaurant with my old high school sweetheart, Rhi. Old flames re-ignited … but were shortly lived. We (I) had changed too much to really give marriage a go, although we came very close to doing so once again. This was our third go-around since it all started in 1975. It was time to leave it there.

Upon returning from "Det 151", we were back in pre-inspection mode. The SAC Inspection General visit came in October to evaluate us on our wartime aircraft generation, mobility exercise, and operational readiness. We performed in an outstanding manner. As tough as it was, we were always operating in a wartime mode anyway since our Cold War missions were real. Although the Cold War was often considered "peacetime" at that time, the SR-71 missions required approval from the National Command Authority (the President of the United States or sometimes the Vice-president or Secretary of Defense). It was a complicated process.

Meanwhile, President Reagan and General Secretary of the Communist Party of the Soviet Union Mikhail Gorbachev had a summit in Reykjavik, Iceland to discuss dismantling of nuclear weapons. Although no agreement was reached, just to see them talk was a new turning point in Cold War relations. Earlier that year, new terms emerged from Gorbachev such as "Perestroika" (Soviet restructuring) and "Glasnost" (era of openness) … maybe there was hope in the future.

By November, Angela and I were talking again. We really missed each other (and Mikey too). Although it was nice being back home with her family, and school was going well, it just wasn't the same. The eight-month break was a wake-up for us and we were still very much in love and really belonged together. She came back out to California to see me for a visit in November and we picked up like nothing changed. Despite the aftermath of the flood and supporting all those Blackbird missions, all the family and life plans were still there … we were still engaged. She went back to Tennessee for the Christmas holidays as we discussed wedding plans. We were finally putting a very tumultuous 1986 behind us!

But just as we were planning their return from Tennessee back to California, fate would redirect us once again. Disheartened, I received orders for a one-year tour … back to Korea. After a joyous two-week reunion in Tennessee in February and time together as a family once again, we had planned a wedding for August of 1987 as part of my six-month mid-tour leave. The good thing was that I had a follow-on assignment back to Beale Air Force Base in California … so off to Korea I went after a brief stop to attend my sister's wedding in Colorado.

OSAN AIR BASE, REPUBLIC OF KOREA, 1987

During this time, I learned that Beale had earned an "Outstanding" rating during its recent SAC Air Force Maintenance Standardization and Evaluation Team visit. The 9th Strategic Reconnaissance Wing had also won the Riverside Trophy as the "Best Overall Wing" in the 15th Air Force for the second time in six years and the 15th Air Force "Outstanding Reconnaissance Unit" Award a second year in a row. In addition, Beale Air Force Base was selected as the U.S. Air Force Commander-In-Chief's "Installation Excellence" Award winner. I was so proud to leave Beale after serving six years there on such a high notes of success!

Upon arriving to Osan in February of 1987, I returned to my former unit working U-2 aircraft as I did in 1983, some 4 years earlier. I directly supported continuous U-2R operations of two on-station aircraft patrolling along the 38th parallel demilitarized zone (DMZ). It felt like I quickly picked up where I left off with U-2 missions and maintenance. In the context of the Cold War, I was just switching theatres of operation. The North Korean leader was still there too. Interestingly, Kim Il Sung fled to Manchuria as a boy to escape Japanese rule during World War II, joined a communist youth organization, and entered into the Korean guerilla resistance. The Soviet Union noticed his potential and sent him back to Russia for military and political training within the Communist Party. He returned to Korea to lead a Korean contingent as a Major in the Soviet Army. After the Japanese surrender in 1945, Kim would help set up a Soviet style communist provisional government which became North Korea in 1948. He would then launch the invasion into South Korea in 1950 hoping to unify the country by force, not elections. The active war ended with a cease-fire in 1953 and the stalemate stayed in place as he remained in control (until his death in 1994). Such was the backdrop of constant war-posturing during my time there in 1983 and 1987.

Meanwhile "Team Spirit '87," a joint military exercise of U.S. and South Korean military forces were commencing, which meant a huge influx of more troops and opposing force maneuvers. The North Koreans continued their probes and infiltration efforts, which resulted in real world casualties. This constant state of war was a normal way of life in the south. But it was far better than the communist life of misery in the north. "Freedom is not free" and we all knew it. It was very visible there. Meanwhile, our U-2s flew daily sorties and the long maintenance and support hours went with it. But now, I was the lead egress technician with a specialist from Beale who rotated out every 65 days, just as I did in 1983. It did require removing the ejection seat and rocket catapult to facilitate other cockpit maintenance, then inspect and reinstall these items.

As a maintainer at a detachment, we did more than just our specialized job. I performed egress and other aircraft maintenance assisting crew chiefs. We were cross-utilized, or CUT-trained in a variety of areas. "Wing walking" as aircraft marshallers ensured the long wings cleared the RF-4 revetments during taxiing, installing the "pogos" (wing wheels) after landing, or a few of us sitting on the left wing so the right wing would be raised enough to clear a taxiway light on a left turn … if too close. We'd constantly run "chase" in the maintenance truck following the chase car "talking down" a U-2 … all were a part of the daily adventure. I even got to ride as "shot gun" (right seat) in the Chevrolet El Camino, as the driver, another U-2 pilot, sped down the runway and talked-down the plane to touch-down. I got to hear the entire radio communication first-hand and experience the whole speedy chase ride. We also celebrated a flying milestone. Our U-2R, #10329 completed its 10,000th flying hour on 24 February 1987. But I also had other additional duties that made days long such as being the detachment mobility NCO, "Cat Walk" scheduler, and "Oscar" caretaker and feeder.

But we also had fun too! As an egress guy, I worked with explosives, and as such I'd often go down town ("to the Ville") to a local bar called "Skinny Mom's" … where other "Ammo" or weapons guys often would hang out. One tradition was drinking out of an "Ammo Bowl" or helmet, depending how many were in the group. The metal or plastic bowl was filled with Korean Soju, Backus-D (a chaulky tasting drink), and a few other concoctions, with ice. Then 10 guys with straws would suck it dry! Well, it didn't take too many of those "slurpees" to take effect. Well, a few of these bowls would end up back at the Det as "war trophies." Sure enough, during one such libation, we got to talking about what a U-2 would look like with propellers on it … then voila, a couple of broom sticks and pieces of cardboard, and it became a reality! Our U-2 looked pretty cool in that configuration (but then we wondered what the intelligence folks and local spies were reporting when they saw it)!

But I also got to work with our Physiological Support Division (PSD) crew. They were the enlisted medical team that served as life support for Blackbird pilots. Their job was to ensure the flights suits were serviceable and assist the pilot in suiting-up. They tested and maintained the pressure suit's components such as the oxygen, communication, air conditioning, and pressure regulated items. It was similar to a space suit that astronauts used due to the high altitudes and cold temperatures. But the pressure suit was actually for the pilot's survival in the event of ejection or rapid decompression. The PSD team would escort the pilot to the aircraft then connect-up his suit fittings to the cockpit. I had the pleasure to "suit up" one time when the PSD team needed to perform tests and pressure checks. Being an ejection seat guy, I gained an appreciation of how the systems worked in concert with the survival kit and parachute systems that connect to the escape system.

Then on 12 June 1987, President Reagan went to West Berlin in West Germany and delivered his famous speech at the Brandenburg Gate that would resonate throughout Europe and the world. He called for the General Secretary of the Communist Party of the Soviet Union to open the Berlin Wall. His one line, "Mister Gorbachev, tear down this wall" would become synonymous with hope of ending the Cold War. But there would be no such "hope" one-liners in the Koreas. Demonstrations soon erupted as Seoul, South Korea was selected for the 1988 Summer Olympics and the North was constantly trying to disrupt any progress of the construction of facilities for those events.

On 15 and 16 July, Typhoon Thelma hit South Korea causing floods and landslides that killed over 92 people, 31 missing, 170 injured, and left 160,000 homeless. On Osan, more than 11 inches of rain fell in 36 hours. The deluge was the worst that part of the country had seen in many years. The binjo ditches (Korean open drainage systems) overflowed on base and our aircraft shops and hangars were flooded, so we went to emergency mode moving tools and equipment to higher areas. Three feet of water was challenging enough. But it was only a year ago that I had wrestled with a far greater flood experience and those memories definitely floated back to me. I remembered and reached back to the levee runs I did in California and started running again. This time I pushed to the 6-mile distance, running the slightly raised perimeter of the airfield gazing at the miles of surrounding flooded rice paddies. I'd wave at the South Korean soldiers still manning their muddy outer gun sites. As the waters receded, we quickly carried on with scheduled operations including an airshow at Osan that featured the Air Force Thunderbirds. Airshows were great but it meant a large amount of work and security concerns, especially with on-going U-2 operations at that location.

The Republic of Korea (ROK) soldiers were always ready to respond for our airfield defense in all weather. Their positions were like mini islands in the mud. It was easy to imagine the conditions here in 1950 and '53. But being on alert posture was the norm … but then another incident would occur, and things would intensify again. One such incident was when a North Korean military vessel attacked two South Korean fishing boats in international waters sinking one of them with 13 people on-board. The North insisted it was spying and had rammed one of its vessels. Such were the issues that the United Nations Command constantly battled with. But with the backdrop of the pre-Olympic setting, South Korea was becoming an economic power and a symbol of success in the free world. These were signs of strength that could weaken the communist ideology … just as Reagan's speech was in Europe.

Meanwhile, I was recognized for saving the Air Force over $23,000 annually through four suggestions through the Air Force Suggestion program that I had submitted while at Beale. I had suggested a change to removal procedures on the U-2 canopy jettison thrusters allowing for their re-use after removal. The other three suggestions were also for SR-71 and U-2 egress systems in improvements and simplified less-costly procedures. I was quite proud of these achievements and it reminded me why I was a SAC Master Technician.

By this time, six months had passed and I was ready for my 4-week mid-tour leave to Tennessee … and a real nice wedding in August. After all we had been through, we were finally getting married. At 28 years old and a long run at being single, a much needed vacation and family time with Angela and Mikey had arrived. But time flew by quickly again. The military lifestyle and the call of my Cold War duties would quickly remind me of other obligations that still had to be fulfilled. I would go on a return trip back to Korea for my remaining six months of duty there.

Upon returning to Korea, I resumed my normal pace of operations. Ironically, during this time three of us that were stationed at Bitburg in the late 70's were now stationed in Korea in the late 1980's … thus a reunion was planned. As such, in September, "Ace" flew in from Michigan to join us. "Ace" (Keith), "Hans" (Lou), "Gypsy" (Bruce), and I ("LeBeau") had an awesome time! Now in our 20s and no longer in our teens, we still had not changed much in our partying ways … and yes, the nicknames were derived from our time at Bitburg. We went to see local Osan area historical battle sites, museums, and stadiums for the upcoming 1988 Olympics in Seoul, and a somber visit to the DMZ in Panmunjom. A most memorable visit was at the site of the 1976 tree-chopping incident that had almost kicked off renewal of the war. Although I had visited this site in 1983 and saw the remains of the tree that still stood there, I didn't realize how close it was to the "Bridge of No Return" in the Joint Security Area. That bridge was used for the exchange of prisoners at the end of the Korean War. The Military Demarcation Line between North and South Korea runs right through the middle of that bridge.

Known as the Korean axe-murder incident, it involved the killing of two U.S. Army officers who were overseeing the cutting down of a poplar tree that was blocking the line of sight between a checkpoint and an observation post. The team was confronted by a North Korean group and told to cease the tree trimming. Using axes used by the tree-trimmers the group bludgeoned the two officers. Three days later, American and South Korean forces launched Operation "Paul Bunyan" (named after the fabled tree-cutter). With a show of force and the cut down of most of that tree, it intimidated North Korea enough into backing down. The stump was replaced with a monument in 1987, which I again got to see, but this time in a museum.

Certificate of Entry Into North Korea
Joint Security Area

THIS CERTIFIES THAT

TSGT DAVID L. HAMEL

DID

CROSS THE MILITARY DEMARCATION LINE
INTO COMMUNIST NORTH KOREA AS AN
OFFICIAL GUEST OF THE UNITED NATIONS
COMMAND SECURITY FORCE-JOINT SECURITY
AREA, PANMUNJOM, KOREA, ON THIS ___26___
DAY OF ___SEPTEMBER___, 19 _87_____

LTC, IN
COMMANDING
UNCSF-JSA

144

All the good food, beverage, and freedoms enjoyed, again stood in great contrast to the reality and seriousness at the DMZ. A simple line across the land and on the table and floor was the 38th parallel … a clear line between freedom and communism. Stern faced North Korean soldiers stood at-the-ready as we witnessed as observers in uniform. And much like our Octoberfest trip in 1979 in Germany, our side-visit to the Dachau concentration camp site was another clear reminder of why we serve. Almost 10 years later we were together and greatly reminded why we will always be comrades, buddies, and bonded together in service, in OUR Cold War life. After our reunion, it was back to work and our U-2 missions steadily continued. By this time, Det 2 had reached the 4,000th sortie plateau on 14 November 1987 and we celebrated another mission milestone on helping keep South Korea free … and communism in check.

Our short-lived celebration was followed by a reminder of how quickly freedom-haters would respond. On 29 November, Korean Air Flight 858 exploded in mid-air over the Andaman Sea on its second stop-over to Bangkok, Thailand on its way back to Seoul, South Korea. North Korean agents had planted a bomb in a storage bin on a Boeing 707 killing all 115 on-board. The attack was an act of terror in an attempt to sabotage the 1988 Olympics in Seoul since they lost the bid to co-host the event in Pyongyang, which again almost resulted in conflict on the Korean peninsula. We all felt its impacts once again. We were always on the brink of resumption of full-scale war with no end in sight it seemed.

Meanwhile, on 15 August on the 42nd anniversary of Korea's liberation from Japan (Independence Day) the newly opened Independence Hall of Korea was a must-see, as my time was winding down in this country. I got to visit it 3-months later after its grand opening and it is the largest exhibition hall in South Korea ranging from prehistoric times to dynasty era times, but largely focuses on the independence movements during the Japanese Colonial Period (1910-1945). The most visible item is a twin tower-like monument to the nation representing the wings of a soaring bird and two hands joined in prayer.

On the other end of the Cold War spectrum, the Intermediate Range Nuclear Forces Treaty (INF) was signed on 8 December 1987. This agreement by the United States and Union of Soviet Socialist Republics was to eliminate an entire class of nuclear weapons, largely intermediate and shorter-range land based and cruise missiles within specific ranges. This would have big implications world-wide, but especially so in Europe. The Cold War as we knew it was beginning to thaw … albeit just a little bit.

Meanwhile, the South Korean Presidential elections were underway on 16 December. During all the turmoil of events through the summer nationwide, protests were occurring in the background, which were known as the "June Struggle." On election day, all soldiers and police were put on maximum alert as commanders predicted communist North Korea would attempt to disrupt the voting. At the same time, senior members of the Korean People's Army / Chinese People's Volunteers had said that United Nations Council (UNC) naval vessels entered North Korean territorial waters and that SR-71s were "presumably" flying over the north. Meanwhile, the UNC senior member (Rear Admiral William T. Pendley) dismissed the charges as propaganda and that no armistice violations occurred. He also stated that "as you have been told many times before, the flight of the SR-71 is so carefully controlled that there is no possibility whatsoever that it can violate your side's legal airspace" (Stars & Stripes newspaper, Dec 1987) … you decide.

Meanwhile, the SR-71s flying out of Kadena Air Base in Okinawa Japan had their own mission taskings to various parts of the world, and Korea was definitely one of their areas of operations. But as a sister detachment from Mother Beale, we all kept abreast of all our worldwide operations … as we all supported aircraft maintenance worldwide also. Such was the Blackbird community. Globally, we fought the Cold War anywhere. Our quiet motto, "Kill 'em with Kodak!" (in reference to the Kodak camera film company).

Despite all the chaos and craziness in the real world as we knew it, I continued my extra duties as Mobility NCO constantly adjusting our detachment "bug-out" plan in case of invasion or typhoon evacuation. I was also, "Oscar" the Black Cat's caretaker and "Cat Walk" scheduler. The real "Oscar," Black Cat I, was the mascot of the unit who usually spent most of his time sleeping in the commander's office. I knew and fed Oscar briefly during my 65-day tenure in 1983. He was a bit wacky at times as his legendary history was a bit unique. From what I understood, he had a flight in a U-2 in 1978. He got an orientation or "check flight" in a special cage set up in the camera bay of the airplane. Well, he wouldn't be "quite right" after that experience and he would go into hiding at the sound of each mission engine start-up.

Oscar I, was also castrated along the way as his "nuts" were preserved in a jar and proudly displayed. I don't remember if they were on display at the Det office or at the Black Cat lounge, but it probably went back and forth to elude capture (and it's reported Oscar I went AWOL or MIA somewhere in late 1984 and never located). However, in 1985, Oscar II was acquired. By the time I returned in 1987, I assumed his caretaker duties once again. But I needed Oscar's "official" approval of my Cat Walk schedule before releasing it, as tradition dictates, as he out-ranked me as approving official! His signature block was "OSCAR I. BLACKCAT, 1Lt (First Lieutenant), Cat Walk Coordinator." I never did find out why his middle initial was "I"… and not sure what became of him after my departure in 1988, (but it's been later reported that he went AWOL or MIA in 1990 when he did not return from one of his "forays" … much like Oscar I, did).

Oscar II, 1987

DEPARTMENT OF THE AIR FORCE
HEADQUARTERS 9TH STRATEGIC RECONNAISSANCE WING (SAC)
BEALE AIR FORCE BASE, CA 95903-5300

REPLY TO
ATTN OF: CCM

6 February 1987

SUBJECT: CAT WALK

TO: ALL DETACHMENT BLACKCATS

The following is a list of establishments for tonight's CAT WALK.

BOOGIE HOUSE 0900-0930

GOLD STAR 0930-1000

A-FRAME 1000-1030

2ND FLOOR/MOCKOLAI HOUSE........ 1030-1100

TORCH 9 1100-1130

EAGLES 1130-1200

HAPPY HOUR!!! 1200-UNTIL

Oscar says "Be Careful and have a Good Time and Get Home Safe."

OSCAR I. BLACKCAT, 1Lt, USAF
Cat Walk Coordinator

As I entered 1988, and my time in Korea was nearing its end, the long work hours, partying with the guys, and still getting in some run time kept me stable. I closed out a great year as the 1988 New Year's Eve baby on my next-to-last cat-walk. As cold as it was, my buddies selected me to lead my final charge as Cat Walk Scheduler into the new year … and what a classic night it would be as I would earn my highly coveted "100 Missions Over Songtan" patch. It would soon be someone else's turn to assume those duties, with vigor I might add, as my time in Korea was "short" (a term of endearment meaning "almost time to leave").

Those months zoomed by too as Angela and I planned our move back to California as I was expecting to receive my assignment orders soon in January. Meanwhile my old unit back at Beale was recognized as the best maintenance squadron in SAC! The 9th Field Maintenance Squadron received the Air Force Outstanding Unit Award for those assigned to it in 1986 and 1987. Of all my maintenance activity at that time, my Air Force Suggestion Program Awards probably factored in that achievement too. Hopefully, I'd be returning to that same squadron.

But as military life goes, my assignment was changed during my last month in-country. With the AIDs epidemic spreading worldwide, a new requirement was added to our out-processing checklist before re-locating … an AIDS test. AIDs is an Acquired Immune Deficiency Syndrome that comes from the Human Immunodeficiency Virus (HIV). It damages the immune system making it easier to get sick and die. It is largely spread through sexual contact. A negative blood test was now required. The blood sample testing had to be sent to the U.S. Army Garrison Hospital in Yongsan, near Seoul. That added 30 days in-country to get the results back. How do you explain that to a newlywed wife? Despite a negative result, that delay resulted in my assignment being changed. There would be no return to Beale. But I did return stateside for some leave time in Massachusetts and Tennessee to visit family with Angela and Mickey. However, our next move was to Kadena Air Base on Okinawa in March; a tropical island 640 miles south of Japan, only 70 miles long and 7 miles wide, and a new trajectory would begin for all of us, once again.

KADENA AIR BASE, OKINAWA JAPAN, 1988

We would remain in the Blackbird world and "Det-hop" once again as part of the "Mother Beale" family. I went from Detachment 2, 9 SRW Korea to Detachment 1, 9 SRW Okinawa and remained in the Pacific theatre directly supporting operational missions. The long reach of the SR-71 from Okinawa since the 1960s ensured continued real-world missions. As such, we directly supported SR-71A missions of two on-station aircraft during routine Cold War Southeast Asia standoff reconnaissance sorties largely in the Russia, China, Vietnam, & Korea regions … and those missions continued. There were only two of us in the egress shop. I was the Senior Technician with an E-4 "Buck" Sergeant and we kept busy supporting aircraft launches and performing scheduled and unscheduled maintenance. I also served as the Real Property Facility Manager of our $1.4M SR-71 maintenance complex, which included our "T-Hangar" facilities, supply, fuel storage, and area grounds. I also coordinated four engineering contracts valued at $1.8M. The building was shaped like a "T" with the four aircraft bays forming the top facing the flight line where the aircraft would taxi out to the runway. We were located on the "SAC" side of the runway across from the F-15 units, but we did have a unit near us that flew the Airborne Early Warning and Control System (AWACS). That unit flew the Boeing E-3 Sentry, which is a flying radar system that detects ships, vehicles, aircraft, and incoming missiles. It detects and tracks targets and manages the battle space. It's very distinguishable with its rotating radome on top of the aircraft. With increased surveillance of North Korea and show of force in South Korea due to the upcoming 1988 Summer Olympics in Seoul, military activity also remained active in its surrounding waters to provide South Korea the earliest possible warning of trouble as political exploitation from North Korea continued.

Meanwhile in March, an SR-71 tested Soviet air defenses when it skirted Soviet territory over the Sea of Okhotsk. The U.S. detected 15 Soviet planes had scrambled attempting intercepts of the Spyplane. The Soviet air defenses had been upgraded after a teenager landed a small plane in Red Square which had humiliated the Kremlin, a fortified complex in the center of Moscow … it was also the same region where KAL 007 wandered unchallenged for 70 minutes in 1983 before being shot down.

(Creative Commons)

During this 20th anniversary year of the arrival of the SR-71 to Okinawa we celebrated with great fanfare (1968-1988). Angela and Mickey quickly settled in and we were off to a great new start on a tropical island! It was a 3-year tour so we set our sights on goals that we had put on hold in California and in Korea. We were all pretty excited in 1988 to re-start a new life, as newlyweds, and maybe soon start a family. I was also working a dream assignment on the SR-71 and I was able to take one college class each semester. Angela was working and Mikey was doing very well in school. We had also visited island attractions such as the Southeast Botanical Gardens, Cape Maeda and Zampa, and walked around the ancient Zakima, Nakagusuka, Katsuren, and Aegena Castles. Live snake shows at the Gyokusendo Habu Park where also always entertaining. As such, we got to see a real "Habu" snake, the SR-71's nickname. The Okinawa Peace Memorial Hall was a must-see and a reminder of the cost of war. The seaside sunsets at the nearby U.S. Army's Torii Beach were relaxing. By April, I had graduated from the Community College of the Air Force earning an Associate in Applied Science degree in Aircraft Accessory Systems Technology. By summer, the annual Kadena Karnival was in full swing celebrating the 4th of July, where plenty of Okinawan vendors served up fried octopus and yakisoba in addition to hot dogs and hamburgers. This first year was great for all of us!

While our missions were focused on Cold War target areas, there were operational missions that did pop up. During this time, the Iran-Iraq War was complicating the geo-political landscape of the Middle East. It lasted from September 1980 to August 1988, 8 years. That war started when the Iraqi army invaded Iran. Both had a long history of border disputes and further motivated by fears that the Iranian revolution of 1979 would inspire an insurgency in Iraq. But Iraq only made minimal progress before being repelled back into Iraq. It ended with no changes in borders but cost about a half a million Iraqi and Iranian soldier's lives and another similar number in civilian casualties.

(Shutterstock)

It was during this time that the Shatt al Arab waterway was considered an important channel for both states oil exports. This led to skirmishes against merchant vessels in the Persian Gulf and Strait of Hormuz from 1984 to 1988 that ended in a cease-fire. The U.S. intervened in 1986 to protect Kuwaiti oil tankers, which led to engagements with Iran. This led to the "Tanker War" when the U.S. then reflagged Kuwaiti tankers making them eligible for U.S. Navy escort. From a Cold War perspective, the U.S. sought to minimize the Soviet role in the Gulf. It became known as Operation "Earnest Will," one of the largest U.S. naval operations since World War II. But in 1987, Iran sought to deploy Chinese made CSSC-2 "Silkworm" missiles with much larger warheads, which became its first anti-ship cruise missiles. This led to two 11-hour SR-71 flights in July and August from Kadena (64-17967 and 64-17975) to the Persian Gulf during these "Silkworm" missile detection missions. Two more similar flights would follow in 1988 (64-17979 and 64-17974). These long duration, high priority missions did reveal the presence of the missiles in Iran and massive military items in the Gulf that gave warning to the U.S. Navy. These missions gained quiet fame. But it wasn't enough, as the Pentagon announced scrapping four of the nine SR-71s at Beale and the program by 32%. It would soon be felt at Det 1, but not without a nice "Habu Team" picture in June with both aircraft. By July, one aircraft would be recalled to Beale (64-17979). It was the beginning of the drawdown of our Blackbird mission here.

But the summer continued on well with the family. We went to see the Ryukya Mura Habu Center and nearby underwater observatory. We loved to drive around the Okinawan countryside visiting pineapple groves in my Mazda Bongo van and camp out and snorkel along the coasts and up to Hedo Point, the northernmost point of the island. By September, we enjoyed a huge Okinawan event at the Oban Festival. Meanwhile the 1988 Summer Olympics had begun in South Korea. During this time, there was a brief visit to the island from my Dragon Lady family. We would support a U-2R with a special hump on its back we sometimes called "Willie the Whale" in the U-2 community. An odd sight to see, it was actually configured with a satellite communication pod called Senior Span, which was high-tech during its time. As with other aircraft, it sometimes came with its own tail art.

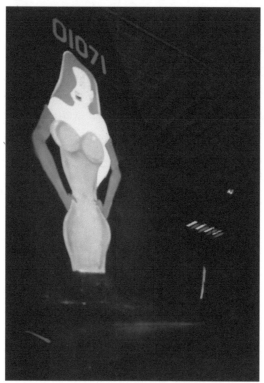

KADENA AIR BASE, OKINAWA JAPAN, 1989

By fall, Angela, Mikey, and I would continue our travel forays to the Okinawa Zoo, Nakagin Castle - Motobu, the Tropical Dream Center, and the Aquapolis. We would also experience Typhoon Nelson with torrential rain and wind gusts up to 100 miles an hour in November, and a 4.8 earthquake on the Richter scale. Both were common and frequent events in the region. A severe drought also occurred as we kept containers of water at home during a water rationing period. In January of 1989, Emperor Hirohito died of cancer at age 87. He held divine status until the end of World War II and endured to reign Japan after 62 years. The coverage brought hard feelings of that war and the 1945 battle of Okinawa for many. It was also a reminder of Japan's defeat, which set the stage of the Cold War in Southeast Asia. It made for a somber time and a new page in history.

By the end of 1988, we decided it was time to conceive a baby. We agreed to cut back the beer intake and quit cigarette smoking to be healthier before conception. I offset these habits by finding a cross-country running club and ran 6 to 8 milers twice a week with the Okinawa Hash House Harriers, which were largely comprised of local Okinawan islanders and American Marines. She scaled back the beers and the smokes … somewhat. We continued our camping and island sight-seeing times during the winter and spring. I continued to win Air Force Suggestion Awards and even won the Kadena Self-Help Award trophy for organizing 20 major facility improvement self-help projects. Life was good! Thus, we planned on going on a week-long Southeast Asia tour from 18 to 29 April to the countries of Singapore, Malaysia, Thailand, Hong Kong (British till 1997-now China), and Macao. In Macao, we could see across no-man's-land into China and watch the communist guards. (Macao was Portuguese territory till 1999-now China). Mitch would not accompany us on this trip. She came off birth control and off we went. In Singapore, Johor, and Bangkok, the evenings were very special. The sights, river cruises, ancient temples, markets, and dinners were fantastic … honeymoon-type moments.

The next day, 21 April, 1989, we headed to Bangkok feeling on top of the world. Nothing can ruin this experience and vacation! But as our military luck would have it, we got word that an SR-71 aircraft had crashed into the South China Sea near the Philippines. The status of the two-man crew was unknown. That left a few of us from the same unit in major angst … especially me, as the senior technician of those two escape systems. Did they eject? If they did, did they parachute safely? If not, I would have a serious conscience check till I knew that they were safe. A million things went through my mind about recent maintenance. Did I overlook anything, despite a confidence check I performed before we left? "This can't be happening!" I thought.

That night we got word that the aircrew had ejected and survived without injury. They were picked up by Filipino fishermen and brought to Clark Air Base in the Philippines. A big relief was sighed, although the cause of the crash was still unknown. But Angela and I were in disbelief again. How could another military event subvert THE prime moment in our lives. It became a bitter-sweet reminder that always seemed to loom over us.

The rest of our trip went well and we had a good time in Hong Kong and Macao, but the constant updates and play-by-play of the aircraft recovery were a big distracter that greatly overshadowed our good time. After all, the Cold War was still not over and we knew enemy subs and trawlers would be trying to collect valuable intelligence about that spyplane. The pilot, Lieutenant Colonel Dan House and the reconnaissance systems officer (RSO) Blair Bozek were safe and very thankful. When we returned to Kadena, I was in full aircraft recovery operation mode. The Navy was able to salvage the aircraft in three major sections and bring it to White Beach Naval Station on Okinawa on the U.S.S. Beaufort. I worked with the Explosives Ordinance Disposal team (EOD) to de-arm any unfired escape systems explosives, and only the RSO seat was recovered. But I was engulfed in those operations and very long work days in the following months. At Kadena, Sergeant Clarence Campbell III and I continued the egress item recovery in the hangar. After the SR-71 crash, a replacement aircraft was sent (64-17962), and we continued to do operational missions. Sometimes a maintenance issue would occur and the aircraft would have to divert somewhere. As such, I was part of a maintenance team that would board a tanker, in June. Ironically, an SR-71 with an engine problem made an emergency approach and successfully landed at Clark Air Base in the Philippines. But our experienced maintenance team made the repairs and we returned to Kadena within a few days.

Meanwhile, I had an impressive explosives safety program that led to our selection as winner of the 5th Air Force's "Tip of the Spear" Safety Award for the Pacific Air Forces Command (PACAF) for 1988. I graduated from Central Texas College receiving my second Associates degree, and was also selected for promotion to Master Sergeant! Angela, Mikey and I would resume our campouts and trips and took a boat trip to Ie Shima Island. We all seemed to be continuing to do well.

By this time, the Cold War was changing rapidly. By 1989, the USSR was facing economic difficulties with a costly arms race and liberal reforms causing major problems. The 1979 invasion of Afghanistan finally came to an end in February, followed by the Solidarity Party's decisive victory in Poland in June. There was also the end of communism in Hungary in October, the Berlin Wall coming down in Germany in November, followed by the fall of communist regimes in Czechoslovakia and Romania. These were followed by mostly peaceful revolutions sweeping the Soviet bloc states of Eastern Europe. Internal strife within the USSR would become post-Soviet separatist conflicts. But this also added challenges for the need, or continuation of, the SR-71 program. As such, the Department of Defense eliminated funding for the Blackbird. Meanwhile in November, the Space Shuttle Discovery was launched carrying a high-tech spy satellite. Vast improvement in satellite capability such as "Lacrosse" and "KH" series items were also a big factor, along with the Titan 4 rocket. It was the beginning-of-the-end of the Detachment life as we knew it at Kadena. It appeared 1990 would be a year of big change, for all of us it seemed.

During the summer after our South East Asia Tour in April, we expected that by July Angela would be pregnant. After the SR-71 crash, she began having second thoughts about this whole relationship and military lifestyle once again and became disillusioned about our future. Those thoughts began to fester much like it did in 1986 while at Beale. Through this uncertainty, Angela found that she was not pregnant. We were both surprised and shocked! We couldn't understand why. Were there any medical complications or was it something else? She felt relieved … and I was heartbroken. Feeling helpless once again, I sensed this would be the beginning of another sad trajectory for us. It was becoming evident that this was beyond my comprehension, yet again. Mikey, who was doing so well in school, and karate, and continued running with me, was now having problems in school too, and at home. How can a family disintegrate so rapidly? Scary vibes of us from 1986 began to return.

Despite the good summer we all had, she began an emotional see-saw, and realized she had deep personal issues to resolve. Now numb, and doing the emotional roller-coaster myself, I could not disagree. She went on a retreat to get some personal time to think things over. Feeling helpless, I agreed that it was a good idea. Sometimes loves requires letting go enough to enable some alone time. Upon her return, I gave her space and wanted to support her wherever she was at in her life. I was a good enabler in our relationship and it was very helpful as we did a lot of "walk and talk." Perhaps through this process she could find a new WHY … somewhat as I had in my running program. As helpful as this time was, I felt I was losing her as we entered 1990 … like someone with a terminal illness that just couldn't feel anymore. I wish I could have felt numb in the process too, but I loved her too much. Things were beginning to slip away during the Christmas holidays. During this time, I was trying to survive the emotional roller coaster with her and preserve my relationship with Mikey.

KADENA AIR BASE, OKINAWA JAPAN, 1990

Meanwhile, the ax came down on the SR-71 at Kadena and by late January we prepared for our final one-way aircraft launch to "Mother" Beale. On 18 January 1990, tail #17962 roared down the runway and up into the heavens; it was suddenly the end of a proud era. On the 19th, we did our "Senior NCO Investiture" Ceremony. It was a formal "Dining-In" unit dinner affair as four of us newly promoted Master Sergeants selectees were inducted into the Senior NCO Corps. On 26 January, a "Final Salute" Ceremony to the SR-71 was held at Beale. The Blackbirds would soon be dispersed to museums except for three that were sent to NASA's Ames-Dryden Research Facility at Edwards Air Force Base, in Southern California. The SR-71 also set four speed records in a transcontinental dash as tail #17972 was on its way to the Smithsonian at the National Air and Space Museum arriving at Washington DC's Dulles International Airport.

Meanwhile, Angela was sent off for a medical evaluation at Clark Air Base in the Philippines. By now I was really needing an ear to bend and went to talk to a Catholic priest at the on-base chapel. I was comforted by his words of wisdom but was angered by issues I now had to confront. And I was highly encouraged to attend a twelve-step group program called |Al-Anon Family Support Groups for affected family members, so I could associate with others who may be in similar situations. This lasted a few months as I tried to make the relationship work. We took a ferry and did a campout on Tokashiki Island (20 miles southwest of Okinawa) to try one last revival time together as a family. As we stabilized, Mikey and I also continued to bond and run. He even advanced from a Green, to Blue, to a Purple Belt level in Karate in minimum time. He ran in several Hash runs with me culminating in his first six-mile completion at age 9. I was so proud of him! My effective promotion to Master Sergeant was 1 May. These should've been great times.

Then just as things were beginning to go well, one day out-of-the blue, Angela said she wanted to leave and go back to the states. But we still had 8 months left on my tour of duty. Mikey was now out of school for the summer. I tried to reason and suggested that she go home for the summer in Tennessee, rethink things, and return in the fall in time for the boy to resume school. But she made it clear … she was NOT returning. After constant pleading, I now had a decision to make. I was not going to leave business unfinished. She had a history of unfinished business in previous relationships and of sabotaging successful moments in her life … so I asked to part ways. Something I surely did not want and would never do … but it was now a matter of self-preservation. It had to be done or we'd just prolong the inevitable and turn this relationship from sadness to real anger … we both didn't want that … the cycle had to be broken. We agreed on everything and quickly settled in June. Now I had 30 days to move out of base housing and into the dorms. We hastily packed up and boxed her and the boy's items. Mikey and I would have one more great weekend together on Yoron Island with the Hash House Harriers.

I was so proud of him and loved him, and he didn't want to leave me. But I had to explain that he must be with his mother. I had a heart-to-heart talk with this now 10-year old boy, a dad and step-son talk. It was difficult to explain in child terms that although I may not be his father, I will always be his special dad. I could at least leave him with that thought to carry him through another day. I then brought them to the airport, and they were gone. My hopes and dreams for our family also gone with them in disbelief once again.

And as if I wasn't rattled enough, the frequent earthquakes and tremors, up to 20 a year, continued. They often were 4.0 up to 6.0 in magnitude, one of which unhinged a huge hangar door. Luckily, it lodged against an aircraft tow vehicle. I was the facility manager, so it added a few extra duties to my days. As I transferred the SR-71 facilities and grounds complex over to its new owners, I stayed focused as best as I could and maintained stellar performances at work. But there were hidden costs to our Cold War story that she and I had missed along the way … now it had arrived. She departed along with the legacy of the SR-71. I too had to adapt with the times. After I transferred the SR-71 facilities and property management over to the 33rd Rescue Squadron, a helicopter unit, I was re-assigned to the F-15 side of the base, home to the 18th Tactical Fighter Wing.

I was assigned to the 18th Component Repair Squadron and became the egress shop chief managing the F-15C & D model fighters with 22 technicians maintaining 84 aircraft. It was a new era for me to leave the Strategic Air Command after 10 years and now I became part of the Pacific Air Command Air Forces (PACAF). But before doing so, our Detachment commander Colonel Lee Shelton undertook the task to leave a Habu memorial plaque on "Habu Hill." It was an aircraft viewing area near the flight line where people would gather to watch the Blackbird take-off. He pooled together any leftover "slush" funds to construct it. It read,

"This vantage point is dedicated to the magnificent SR-71 Blackbird, known worldwide as the Habu – an Okinawan cobra of black, sinister appearance, great stealth, and lightning fast strike. The first SR-71 arrived at Kadena Air Base on 9 March 1969, and the last aircraft departed on 21 January 1990. Throughout those twenty-two years, the Habu roamed Pacific skies unchallenged, in war and peace, to ensure the freedom of the United States and her allies. Habu Hill stands as memorial to the SR-71, the special men and women who sustained its strategic reconnaissance mission, and to all people who gather here and know that jet noise is truly the sound of freedom. Sayonara Habu. Detachment One, Ninth Strategic Reconnaissance Wing, 1968 – 1990."

As the Cold War was rapidly winding down and victory was eminent, the mission of the Strategic Air Command would rapidly change with it and the various aircraft that flew its logo. For now, it meant the end of a unique era of the SR-71.

(Creative Commons)

KADENA AIR BASE, OKINAWA JAPAN, 1990 -1991

Despite the SR-71's departure, the regional posture didn't change much. I quickly got certified on the "Eagle" and immediately jumped into a high operations tempo in addition to balancing several egress system modifications. In true form, I would arrive at the start of an operational readiness exercise in the sweltering heat. Inspectors from six major commands evaluated our readiness from a mass aircraft generation and recovery, to a base defense posture and disaster response. We constantly wore our MOPP gear and rapidly responded to attacks and unexploded ordinances (UXOs). With temperatures near 100 degrees and saturated tropical humidity, it was all we could do to stay hydrated as there were heat casualties on the flight line. We often grabbed quick chow at the "Quick Turn" or "QT" café on the flight line or grabbed a "Scarf 'n Barf" from the travelling "Roach Coach." But what a great job Team Kadena did! Although heartbroken of my family loss, it did result in me being better postured to jump into a high optempo transition quickly. Stretched thin from the start, our manning could not keep up with the demand. As a single man now, I could fully devote all my time to being "in the fray."

As such, I was soon selected to lead a maintenance support team for 14 days in August as part of an F-15 package to Anderson Air Force Base that participated in the defense of Guam. It was SAC's 15th Air Force Exercise "Giant Warrior: 'Realm of the West,' '90." The annual exercise often involved B-52s, B-1s, FB-111s, KC-135s, KC-10s, E3 Sentry, HH-3E Jolly Green helicopters, and other assets. Guam is an island in the western Pacific Ocean between Hawaii and the Philippines. It is only 30 miles long and 10 miles wide. It was acquired from Spain after the Spanish-American War in 1898. The Japanese took over the island in 1941 but was re-occupied by the Americans in 1944. During the Cold War, it served as a deterrence against the Soviet Union and utilized as America's forward deployment strategy, which had supported operations during the Korean and Vietnam Wars. "Giant Warrior" exercises from 1988 to '90 displayed a visible presence to world adversaries.

We stayed at "Andy South," an abandoned and dilapidated enlisted barracks with no air conditioning, about 4 miles from the flight line. It did have large fans but wasn't of much comfort after long days on the scorching tarmac in the midst of summer. The area buildings were used for administrative functions by SAC's 3rd Air Division during the Cold War. In between mission take-offs and landings I'd watch in amusement as crew chief's would have "canal races" … basically floating individual cardboard-type cigarette book matches down the ground parking ramp dividers using canteen water and blowing the matches with the wind, and timing the winner at the finish line. Off duty, we enjoyed ourselves at Tarague Beach … I even got a jungle run with the Agana Hash House Harriers!

Upon return, keeping up with the ACES II (Advanced Concept Escape System) egress mods were a challenge, as well as its parts acquisition. One such mod was to enable a "single-motion" action to allow the seat with a piercer to go through the canopy in the event the canopy did not jettison. Another mod was the addition of specialized shoulder harness buckles called SEAWARS. Most problematic during my time at Kadena was the shortage of canopy-actuated initiator coiled lanyards during the single-motion mod. Prior to the mods, the canopy must jettison to allow seat ejection. There was a wire cable connected to the canopy from the initiator, to allow this sequence, that were not allowed any broken strands according to our technical orders (TOs), thereby grounding the aircraft. We would take a good lanyard from one aircraft to install on another back & forth (cannibalize) until there simply were no more good lanyards. It then became how many strands were allowed … well none.

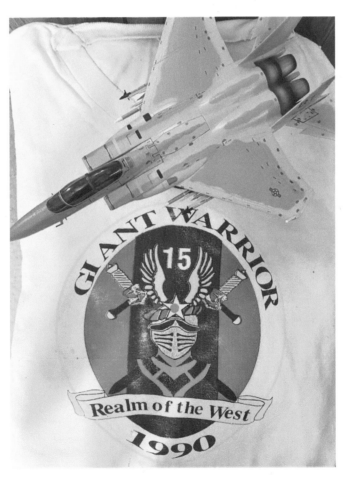

(US National Archives)

My shift supervisors were receiving intense pressure from the Deputy Commander for Maintenance (DCM) to sign off the aircraft forms (781A), to meet sortie rates. But I had instructed my shop personnel not to disregard the TOs. If a system fails and a pilot dies from a failed ejection sequence there would be intense blame and scrutiny of why the TO was not adhered to. The only person who could clear the forms was the DCM. As such, each time an aircraft was grounded for a lanyard fray, the shop would contact me anytime of the day or night, and I would hand carry the forms to the DCM to be reviewed or cleared. Fortunately this only lasted a very short time till a few lanyards arrived and the mods were complete.

After all that intense time, I felt like I was finally able to catch my breath just a little. It was during this time that I met a nice woman from Taiwan at a dinner party. She was the sister of a friend's wife who happened to be visiting on Okinawa. Her name was Kwei-Lun and she invited me to visit her in Taipei. Really needing to get away, I took her up on her offer and spent a week there. Taiwan is officially the Republic of China and is a country in East Asia.

As an island, it shares maritime borders with the Communist People's Republic of China. In keeping with the Cold War history, after the surrender of the Japanese occupation in 1945 much like in Korea and Vietnam, a reunification effort followed. But, a Chinese civil war had resumed between the Chinese Nationalist led by Chiang Kai-shek and the Chinese Communist Party led by Chairman Mao Zedong. By late 1949, the Chinese Communists had defeated the Nationalists on the mainland and formed the People's Republic of China. The Nationalist government evacuated to the island of Taiwan (formerly known as the island of Formosa) and made Taipei the temporary capitol. It claims continued sovereignty over all of China, but the victorious communists proclaimed to be the sole legitimate government of China to include Taiwan. But in the context of the Korean War in the 1950s and the ensuing Cold War, the United States intervened to prevent hostilities between Taiwan and mainland China. By the 1980s, Taiwan became an economic success story much like South Korea. It had avoided Mao's "Cultural Revolution" of the 1960s and '70s and its purges and starvation when millions died. Such was the environment during my visit. Kwei-Lun showed me a most hospitable time with her and her family and was quite the tour guide. We visited the National Palace Museum, Fort San Domingo, the Martyr's Shrine, Sun Yat-Sen Memorial Hall, the Grand Hotel, and a scenic boat ride up the Tamsui River.

(US National Archives)

TAMSUI

I also ran with the China Hash House Harriers (H3) in Taipei, Taiwan … only to do so in the midst of Typhoon Yancy; the scariest cross-country trail run of my life! Our small group was dodging flying debris and bamboo for an hour before finishing and taking cover. Winds gusting up to nearly 100 miles an hour and nearly 18 inches of rain in the mountains surely made this an intense survival run even in the lower less impacted areas of our location. Somehow none of us got hurt, but the storm left 22 dead, destroyed many homes and nearly 5,000 trees. But I was able to recover with other Americans and visit the General Claire L. Chennault American Legion Post 49 in Taipei. Chennault was the legendary leader of the American Volunteer Group, the "Flying Tigers" and its P-40 Warhawk unit in the Republic of China Air Force that quietly helped the Chinese fight the Japanese invasion of China in World War II. My time in Taipei was a splendid time and romantic. But falling in love was not what either one of us wanted or was ready for.

With a few more days left on my leave time, I swung from Taiwan to a brief stop in Fukuoka, Japan then over to Korea to see my long-time buddy Lou, at Taegu Republic of Korea Air Base. We partied together and watched the last F-4 Phantom take-off ending an era of American F-4 presence there. I also completed my Asian Hash House Harriers run tour with the Seoul H3 and the Osan Bulgogi H3 before returning to Kadena. Once I got back to Okinawa, our F-15 unit was gearing up with Operation "Desert Shield" preparations, which started on 2 August 1990. At this point, our egress shop was building up our Mission Support Kits (MSKs) to support any operations scenario leading up to the buildup of troops and defense of Saudi Arabia. By September, some of that pressure we were feeling stemmed from this Gulf War build-up as Saddam Hussein had invaded Kuwait. Later that month, my squadron commander came knocking on my door in the dorms. When a Major shows up at your door in uniform, you know the news is not going to be good. My father Raymond Hamel had died of a heart attack and the Red Cross did the notification. I was suddenly on a flight back to Massachusetts.

Absorbing the shock, I went home to take care of family matters in Massachusetts. The funeral and follow-on activities were bitter-sweet ... nice to return for a visit, but not a "homey-feeling" that I use to have. I realized my life and my world was constantly changing. After my divorce and loss of my father, it was time to prepare for war and I needed to be fit and lead in that effort. When I returned to Kadena, I resumed my workouts and runs. I was lean and in a warrior mind-set. A mindset of self-preservation, personal survival, and a will to win. This culminated in running in my first 26.2 mile marathon. On 9 December 1990, I finished in the Naha Marathon in 4:09:09. With over 18,000 runners, I was in awe that I finished well and in good shape. All I could think of were all of my life events that led me to this point, this victory. One never forgets there firsts at anything ... and that 4:09 finish time would resonate for years to come. Meanwhile, the Christmas holidays were upon us. I felt sad and heartbroken as I dwelled on past Christmases with a wife and step-son that I so dearly loved. I knew letting go would take much more time and distance. But, at least I could keep the tears contained enough to start fresh into the new year. It was still all part of my personal Cold War life which had been finally put behind me ... by leaving it all at the marathon finish line. As I reflected on 1989 and 1990, the Berlin Wall came down, borders opened, and free elections ousted Communist governments everywhere in east Europe. The cost had been high for many during this war of somewhat "silent battles."

As we entered January of 1991, our unit was still scheduled to participate in the "Cope Thunder 91-3" exercise at Clark Air Base in the Philippines. Our aircraft maintenance package went with 16 aircraft and pilots of the 44th Tactical Fighter Squadron as an operations-maintenance composite team. We also associated with Osan's F-16s as well as F-16s from Thailand, the Royal Thai Air Force. Launching and recovering successful air-to-air superiority training sorties was an enjoyable adventure.

Meanwhile, the United Services Organization (USO) was set to entertain the base with a very special singer. As part of his "Stormfront" Tour, Billy Joel was a big star in the 1980s with hits such as "Piano Man," "Tell Her About It," and "Uptown Girl." But his release of, "We Didn't Start the Fire," had a strong Cold War flavor in its lyrics and became a big hit during this time. I was at the base billets called the "The Mabuhay Inn," the night Billy Joel's airplane landed at Clark. I was alone on the second floor waiting for the elevator door to open. When it did, there stood a short man with big bulging eyes, by himself. We stared at each other, then I asked him if he was Billy Joel. He said yes, and that he had just got off the plane and the officers wanted to snag him right away to go to the Officers Club to play the piano. But he just wanted to get away from everyone for a beer. Well, lo-and-behold, there I stood with a six-pack in my left hand. I lifted it up, tilted my head, and pointed to it with my right hand and asked, "You game?" He said, "Hell yeah!" So there we stood in the elevator lobby area as we introduced ourselves and got into a discussion. Of course, I asked about his wife at the time, Christie Brinkley, who was in Australia for a modeling event. We then got into it about the Yankees and Red Sox rivalries when a few of my other buddies showed up. They brought beer too and a mini-party was on. What an enjoyable time we had! And the concert the next night was fantastic, as we were up in a front row during his outdoor concert on the parade field.

After the concert, the fun time would quickly change. This Cope Thunder exercise, coupled with the recent Giant Warrior exercise on Guam, would set our war preparation stage for what was very soon to come. When Operation "Desert Storm" commenced on 17 January 1991 the air war was on with bombers and cruise missiles too. Our unit quietly transitioned into a reserve-type force. Base personnel were basically locked-down on Clark into a battle readiness posture to support the air war if needed. We all watched the events unfold on TV wondering if we'd get the call. The ground war had also commenced. It's mission was to expel occupying Iraqi forces from Kuwait.

Meanwhile, North Korea did some posturing and sabre rattling of its own to remind us of our primary mission back on Okinawa. But the air war went well and the "100 hour" ground war was supremely successful too. By the 10th of February our F-15 unit returned to Kadena. And by 28 February, the war would be over. Upon return, I resumed my church activity and served as an usher during Sunday Catholic Masses at the base Chapel. But my time in PACAF was getting short. I finished my last Hash House Harriers run completing a total of 168 runs in Asia during my time on Okinawa (as well as in Korea, Philippines, Guam, and Taiwan). I had been selected to bring in the new F-15E Strike Eagles to Clark Air Base and was expecting orders to the Philippines to setup its pre-arrival (bed-down team) operations. But base negotiations with the Philippine government fell-through and I instead received orders to report to Castle Air Force Base in central-east California for April, as the "E"s were being diverted to Elmendorf Air Force Base, Alaska. I would be returning to a Cold War SAC base once again. This time on the legendary B-52G Stratofortress. As it would turn out, it would be good timing for me. In June in the Philippines, Mount Pinatubo, a volcano, would have a cataclysmic eruption. Followed by Typhoon Yunya, these two events would destroy much of Clark Air Base and Subic Naval Station in ash sodden rain. More than 20,000 American personnel would evacuate to Guam and the U.S. as part of Operation "Fiery Vigil." I believe God had saved me from the chaos that would occur. It was time for me to return stateside too. The remaining "Ash Warriors" lowered the American flag for the last time on Clark on 26 November 1991, closing yet another chapter of the Cold War.

CASTLE AIR FORCE BASE, CALIFORNIA, 1991 – 1994

I was assigned to the 93rd Bombardment Wing (Heavy) to the egress shop in the 93rd Maintenance Squadron. I served as the Non Commissioned Officer in Charge (NCOIC) of 12 technicians maintaining 25 B-52G Stratofortress bombers and two T-37A Tweet trainer aircraft. Also known as the Big Ugly Fat Fellow or "BUFF," each B-52 has six escape systems and each Tweet has two. As such, I was there in time to recover Operation "Desert Storm" B-52s returning from various overseas locations. The jets bombed the Iraqi Republican Guard and targeted Iraqi chemical weapons, nuclear, and industrial plants during the war. The last bombers of the 93rd Wing returned by mid-May.

With the Cold War now being officially over, most military bases were still very much drawing down their Cold War posture. Castle Air Force Base was also selected for closure under the Defense Base Closure and Realignment Act during Round II (BRAC '91). But this would take a while and the base maintained its traditional base SAC activity. The gates were closed and traffic stopped when the bugle "Retreat" call was played at the end of the day. Everyone still stood at attention in the base theatre when the National Anthem was played before the movie started. And when the klaxon sounded and base red lights flashed, the SAC alert crews rapidly jumped into their alert response vehicles and raced to the flight line. Everyone stopped and got out of their way! The nuclear posturing was still very serious business and so was the response.

Meanwhile, an SR-71 made its final flight in to Castle Air Force Base on 27 February 1990 (tail # 97960). This aircraft flew over Libya during the 1986 raid. Ironically, I did follow this airplane to Castle … one of many such tail numbers that I had worked on over the years. And like the SR-71, the B-52 mission would drastically change. On 27 September, President H.W. Bush ordered SAC to stop keeping its nuclear-armed BUFFs on around-the-clock alert. These bombers were always poised for retaliatory strikes against the Soviet Union. This affected 11 SAC bases and some 40 bombers. For decades, they stood ready to launch at a minute's notice.

On 1 October 1991, SAC issued an order that all guns on the B-52 be de-activated. That left 102 gunners on Castle to be re-trained to other career fields. The aerial gunner was one of the six-member crew and the only enlisted position on the bomber. Shortly afterward, I attended a ceremony, where four 50-caliber machine guns were removed from the tail end of Stratofortress (tail #92595), placed on a cart, and transferred to the Castle Air Museum. Our aft-facing ejection seat and escape system for that position was now unoccupied. This was a unique reality for our egress shop personnel.

Also in October, the "Castle Golden 50th Anniversary" Air Show had an estimated 200,000 people attend. This would be one of the many "grand finales" that would follow locally and throughout SAC. By the end of the year, I would re-enlist and also set my personal record for running the 26.2 mile marathon in 3:25:19. A 7:50 mile pace for 26.2 miles. In only my third marathon, I was very happy and impressed with that finish time!

Throughout the rest of 1991, I continued to run and attend Al-Anon meetings. I would also resume going to school too. By the fall, I would jump in my van to visit aunts, uncles, and cousins in southern California for the holidays. It was a good year as my life transitioned to a little more personal stability. I was doing well and getting on with life too. This momentum carried into 1992. I ran in all kinds of races: 5Ks, 10Ks, Half and Full marathons. I would jump in my van and travel all over the state camping, fishing, running, and getting on with life. Although I was alone, I was enjoying the solitude, tranquility … and some semblance of serenity.

On 25 December, 1991, at 7:35 pm (Russian time), the 20 X 10 Soviet flag was lowered down from the Kremlin for the last time. On December 26th, the Soviet Union itself dissolved into 15 independent states. They were now Armenia, Azerbaijan, Belarus, Estonia, Georgia, Kazakhstan, Kyrgyzstan, Latvia, Lithuania, Moldova, Russia, Tajikistan, Turkmenistan, Ukraine, and Uzbekistan. The Iron Curtain was suddenly lifted in East Europe. After 45 years, the Cold War was really over.

On 1 June 1992, the Wing was relieved from assignment to SAC and reassigned to the newly formed Air Combat Command (ACC). The tail code was changed from a Castle silhouette to the letters "CA" and carried blue tail stripes. But maintenance continued on and so did its unique challenges.

On one occasion, an in-flight B-52 called in for a 'pop' sound followed by a 'rotten egg' smell near the pilot's seat. We made radio contact with the pilot. The crewmember said he placed his jacket up on top of the seat area. As the plane flew in its orbit trek we viewed the escape system schematics in the shop and determined that he must have lodged the item against the catapult safety pin-pull initiator linkage. Once the linkage is extended far enough it will fire the initiator, an explosive component. Basically, the ejection seat thinks that the upper hatch has jettisoned and gone and is prepared to enable the firing of the seat catapult to eject the seat, should the pilot have a need to initiate egress from the aircraft. The problem is the hatch is still there … oh, that's not good, and very deadly if the seat fires. We then instructed the pilot to install the ejection seat safety pins to safety the seat and make it to home base safely.

On another occasion, a B-52 had a bird-strike somewhere near the cockpit's right side. They called in as an in-flight emergency. When we responded as the aircraft landed, we noticed quite a large hole just below the co-pilot's position near the co-pilot's right foot. Fortunately, it was high enough not injure the co-pilot or ingested into any of the aircraft's right engines. But it was quite the cleanup job for us after we removed the upper co-pilot's hatch and ejection seat. Bird guts and feathers jammed into the side of the aircraft made for a major structural repair job. Such were unusual episodes in aircraft maintenance.

On 1 July, I re-enlisted for another four years. In true Cold War fashion, my commander swore me-in in front of a B-52 on the flight line with members of my egress shop witnessing the event. It was a special day.

"I, David Leo Hamel, do solemnly swear (or affirm) that I will support and defend the Constitution of the United States against all enemies foreign and domestic; that I will bear true faith and allegiance to the same; and that I will obey the orders of the President of the United States and the orders of those appointed over me, according to regulations and the Uniform Code of Military Justice. So help me God."

This version of the Code, which is still in use today, came from Title 10, US Code; Act of 5 May 1960 replacing the wording first adopted in 1789, with amendments effective 5 October 1962.

This was my fourth re-enlistment. Each time, I reflected on what my oath said and reflected on the sacrifices of those that came before me to keep our country free. The military person is in the Profession of Arms. It is an understanding that each member brings their own unique skills to the fight. The cost of those lost during peace-time training, real-world deterrence and posturing, and actual war, is very real.

It was also a transitional time, as I would be selected to serve as the Accessory Flight Superintendent of six maintenance shops (egress, fuels, pneudraulic, electric, aerial reclamation, battery, & tire shops) consisting of 74 technicians maintaining our B-52G and 20 KC-135A and R model tanker aircraft. Aside from maintenance activities, I would become more involved with planning and coordinating schedules and events with Wing staff and production agencies, war planning functions and associated training, and overall management of 41 million dollars in facilities, equipment, and material. It was a big operation but I was up to the challenge. I was feeling good about where I was going in my career and in my personal life.

During this time I aggressively pursued, led, and guided several quality maintenance initiatives on the B-52G and KC-135R hydraulic systems among the various shop personnel saving the Air Force over $420K. We also identified, corrected, and pursued extension of egress ejection seat rocket catapult replacement times that resulted in annual savings of $91K. I had also coordinated improvement of pneudraulic shop auxiliary power unit repairs saving $80K and streamlined undermanned fuel shop operations. These combined efforts and teamwork also reduced our tanker and bomber phased inspection time by two days. These impressive accomplishments led to a very successful Air Combat Command Quality Air Force Assessment of our unit winning the Air Combat Command's "Best" award in the maintenance category. I was also recognized as Senior NCO of the Quarter for the 93rd Field Maintenance Squadron for outstanding management.

Meanwhile, I continued to go to school at night and graduated from the University of Maryland. I went to our class graduation commencement at College Park Maryland and was presented my diploma with a Bachelor of Science degree in Technical Management. I was selected as the Castle Air Force Base "Athlete of the Year" runner-up for the third year in a row. I was finding my niche as a leader on the move!

The Cold War draw-down also meant more era aircraft to various museums. Like the SR-71, an FB-111 would follow me to Castle's Air Museum. Tail number 69-6507 flew in from the 529th Bomb Squadron from Plattsburgh Air Force Base, New York. Ironically, Castle Air Force Base's Vice Wing Commander Colonel Michael Kehoe actually flew that aircraft while stationed at Plattsburgh. I attended a brief ceremony at the museum with yet another tear in my eye knowing that I had maintained that airplane too. More would follow in the years to come to various museums.

As we entered 1993, our G-model bombers were slated for departure from Castle. Many would meet their fate under the terms of the Strategic Arms Reduction Treaty (START). START was a bilateral agreement between the U.S. and Soviet Union on the reduction and limitation of strategic offensive arms that was signed on 31 July, 1991 and entered force on 5 December 1994. But a few months after being signed the Soviet Union dissolved leaving four independent states in possession of strategic nuclear weapons. Those states were Russia, Belarus, Ukraine, and Kazakstan. During that time, Ukraine held nearly one third of the Soviet nuclear arsenal which was the third largest in the world. The START Treaty was a follow-on to the Strategic Arms Limitation Talks (SALT) SALT I of 1972 and SALT II of 1979. These agreements with the Soviet Union were to reduce arms, mainly nuclear capable weapons. However, when the Soviets launched the invasion of Afghanistan during that time, it effectively killed any chance of the treaty being passed by the U.S. Senate. Thus, the treaty remained signed but unratified by the U.S. Senate.

By 1991, with the end of the Cold War, all that had changed. The Air Force made a commitment to eliminate many of its Stratofortresses to stay within the limits set in the agreement. The U.S. could retain 71 B-52s, each equipped to carry 20 cruise missiles. Thus, most of the B-52H models were retained but the older G models were not. Under the START terms with Russia, bombers were selected for destruction. They were sent to the 309th Aerospace Maintenance and Regeneration Group at Davis-Monthan Air Force Base in Tuscon, Arizona. To ensure they would never fly again, the tail sections were chopped-off using a 13,000-pound guillotine dropped from 80 feet. Russian military officers would verify their demise with satellite photos and on-site inspections ... something so unimaginable just a few months ago. As such, Castle's B-52Gs were slated for such an end (some 365 B-52s would be destroyed by 2013).

Meanwhile the rest of 1993 went well for me as I continued running in various races and hiking around Yosemite National Park. Such a gorgeous area to explore. I got involved and supported maintenance on several vintage static display aircraft at the Castle Air Museum in Atwater, California ... just outside the base's main gate. I also served as donations collector and money counter after Sunday Catholic church services at the base chapel. My three-year alone time since my break-up was just what I needed as I focused on my education and career. But a new lady in my life would soon appear before long. She happened to be a Filipina woman who also was starting new a few years after a break-up. Her name is Gloria. Gloria worked at the dining hall on Castle. I would see her as an acquaintance at the gym then sometimes see her with her friends at a karaoke bar ... and yes, we liked to sing! Although she did not drink, her friends tried to get her out to cheer her up ... and be their designated driver. All this resonated with me as I actually had fond experiences with the Filipino people. The people I met there in-country were cheerful and friendly and they loved to cook and eat. She was a church-goer and very much Catholic. A very basic, low maintenance, lovable person, there was nothing to dislike about her.

I had then asked her to go on runs with me. She began to accompany me on marathon weekends as she did the 5K (3.1 mile) races while I ran the 26.2 mile distances. We also had great weekends on Angel Island in San Francisco Bay as I ran the "Romancing the Island" 25K and Lake Merritt Striders 15K in Oakland. We also liked to camp and fish. The communication was often comical trying to understand her version of English. But it was ok to laugh at each other and not take things so serious … live, laugh, love! The running weekends continued. Meanwhile, Castle would host one final air show that summer and in October we prepped and sent Castle bombers to participate in the "Gunsmoke '93" Worldwide Gunnery meet at Nellis Air Force Base, Utah. I would conclude the year with a Senior NCO of the Quarter (Oct-Dec) honors for the 93rd Maintenance Squadron. In November, I was also awarded the USAF Master Munitions Maintenance Badge (Master Sergeant with 5 years in specialty from award of 7-skill level / now called the USAF Master Maintenance Badge). As we entered 1994, Gloria and I resumed weekend running and camping in the marathon van. We got lots of road time. A great mix of trail runs and mountain camping were superb times with Gloria, followed by romantic starry nights by a campfire. Before long, we were engaged!

But with new beginnings, there was also a changeover with the old life … the residue of Cold War life that she and I needed to transition from. As such, on 18 February 1994 a ceremony was conducted on the Castle flight line. It was "A Tribute to the B-52G Stratofortress and the Men and Women Who Contributed to Her Success." As part of that tribute, six aircraft from seven of the remaining B-52 units passed over the Castle airfield in an aerial parade of global power. The units, aside from Castle's 93rd Bomb Wing, were the 5th Bomb Wing from Minot Air Force Base, North Dakota, the 416th Bomb Wing from Griffiss Air Force Base, New York, the 92nd Bomb Wing from Fairchild Air Force Base, Washington state, the 410th Bomb Wing from K.I. Sawyer Air Force Base, Michigan, and the 366th Wing from Mountain Home Air Force Base, Idaho.

This event represented a homecoming as Castle Air Force Base was the first unit to receive B-52s, and most of those aircrews that flew them received their training at Castle. As I stood in formation with the other squadrons, we continued to proudly witness a closing of another Cold War chapter.

Meanwhile, the B-52s continued to depart and the farewells continued. Then on 3 May 1994, aircraft maintainers and guests witnessed the last B-52G taxi and takeoff. Tail #58-0240 became the last B-52G to ever fly in the Air Force. The final roar, and exhaust trail as she lifted off was once again a somber moment. Once she was out of sight, silence set in.

Now that the bombers had left and the tankers were departing for other bases, it was now a matter of where do the personnel go? I had received orders to report to Tyndall Air Force Base in Florida to the F-15 egress shop. But the report date was in June. So we accelerated our plans and set a wedding date for 22 May. After nearly a year in a loving relationship, we grew very comfortable with each other and were married. A beautiful church wedding was performed and done with a mix of Filipino traditions. We had a fantastic ceremony and a weeklong event with friends.

During this time, I was also selected for promotion to Senior Master Sergeant (E-8). Congratulations! ... but that meant I was no longer eligible for the Tyndall position. As my military history would have it, I would be diverted to Altus Air Force Base, Oklahoma. That put a brief chill in my memory banks as I feared this change would once again alter marriage plans. But this time, it didn't really matter. It would be a new beginning for both of us with no baggage ... it didn't matter where. I bid farewells to my Al-Anon friends and received my 6-year, "Be True to Thine Self" coin, closing yet another chapter.

Two weeks later, we left California and spent our honeymoon in Las Vegas then camped along the national parks in Utah, before arriving in Oklahoma. A new adventure and calmer life were to begin for these newlyweds!

POST COLD WAR: IN TRANSITION

My three decades of silent battle had actually drifted into a 4th decade as we entered the 1990s, albeit the end of nuclear war posturing as we knew it. My Cold War life, as I visibly knew it, was virtually over. But in transition to a post-Cold War, the last vestiges of that era would attrition-on as I would remain in that orbit a bit longer. My assignment to Altus Air Force Base to be a flight line expeditor on the Lockheed C-141B Starlifter would keep me with historic vintage Cold War aircraft for a few more years. But many of Castle's KC-135R model tankers would follow me there. However, the KC-135A models were also retired. On 30 September 1995, the 93rd Bombardment Wing was inactivated with the closure of Castle Air Force Base. Conversely, Plattsburgh Air Force Base, New York also closed at that time. These followed Bitburg Air Base, Germany's closure in 1994. Several eastern bloc countries would also give up their Soviet nukes such as Ukraine and Estonia to Russia and became independent. The end of an era in west and east Europe would end.

During the next two years in southwest Oklahoma, I would go through a similar series of events. As I sewed on my Senior Master Sergeant stripes (E-8), I would become the superintendent to consolidate and reorganize the C-141, Lockheed C-5A Galaxy, and KC-135 back-shop support units into one large Sortie Support Flight … only to begin to eventually retire the venerable C-141B afterward. And what a storied aircraft that was. As Castle was the B-52 and KC-135 training base, so was Altus for the C-141, C-5, and now KC-135.

At this point in my career, I had served 18 years. It was the mid-1990s. America was doing quite well. We were finally a peacetime force although humanitarian aid missions would occur. We could finally enjoy our Constitutional freedoms, liberties, and capitalistic life without serious threats of censorship internally and externally, and the media was fairly balanced in their reporting. Our borders were secure as well as our sea and air spaces. The various Cold War country's borders were also self-stabilizing without the totalitarian thumb on them. People went to church, got active in their social organizations, and basically enjoyed some of the goodness of life as we knew it in America. As a Cold War veteran, these were cherished times. We felt no one could take them away, not even internally. We knew our place in history.

By 1996, I would support the arrival of the new C-17A Globemaster III cargo plane, which would became the future workhorse for the Air Force. Six Globemasters would arrive and a new chapter would begin. On 1 October 1998, I was promoted to Chief Master Sergeant (E-9). But in December, I flashed back to an event late on that Christmas Eve night … but it was Cold War 1978 at Bitburg. I was an Airman 1st Class (2-striper) trying to finish up safety-wiring (secure-locking) a canopy remover explosive cartridge (SMDC) line on an F-15 down in Bay 5 area behind the pilot's seat. My Staff Sergeant (E-5) supervisor was handing me a diagonal cutter tool down in the bay. But he kept tugging back on the tool not releasing it. In turn, I kept tugging back getting very pissed and laid into many "F-expletives" at him. However, I did not immediately recognize that it was not he doing the tugging. As I looked up in anger, I then recognized that it was not the 4-striped Staff Sergeant that I'd been swearing at, but an 8-striped shirt-sleeved Chief Master Sergeant that had suddenly replaced him.

As my jaw dropped in amazement, he looked down on me in a stern manner and said, "As soon as you get off-duty tonight Airman, you will proceed to the NCO Club and meet me in the back bar where we shall have a serious chat. Merry Christmas." After he left, my Staff Sergeant had returned, shrugged his shoulders and laughed, and said, "Good luck at the Club. Merry Christmas!" So here we are, two of us egress troops with a couple crew chiefs trying to close down the flight line for the holiday. It was a long 12-hour day, I was tired, stinky, far from home for the holidays, and now demoralized looking forward to an ass-chewing by the maintenance Chief. I get to the club, and there he was with the First Sergeant, both of them with arms-crossed … I knew I was in deep shit. Still in my wrinkled fatigues looking weary he said, "Airman Hamel, you were very disrespectful to me on that airplane tonight. As I contemplate what to do with you, I want to see you eat this bratwurst sandwich and drink this Bitburger Beer." I looked at the First Sergeant, and he returned an affirmative nod.

So here I slowly chowed away on the brat and beer as we looked at each other. My mind was like, "This Chief is fattening me up for the kill." It was like 5 or 6 minutes as I tried to rapidly devour these two items as quick as I could. But it felt like painful eternity as I couldn't imagine what was in his head during this process. Once I took my last swallow of that beer and set it down, the Chief looked at me with a smile and said, "Great job tonight Airman Hamel, you just might be a Chief someday. You have two more beers coming to you. Merry Christmas!" He and the First Sergeant finished their beers and left ... I always wondered why that Chief did that to me. He must have seen something in me ... or maybe a reflection of him during his Airman years. But twenty years later, Chief Master Sergeant Hamel now gazed at the Altus flight line, then radioed-in the C-17 flight line expediter. A Master Sergeant (E-7) arrived in his maintenance truck for immediate pickup, as we were attempting to wind down the flight line for the holidays.

I pointed to a C-17 that had a crew chief standing in the nose wheel-well attempting to service the tire or strut. The airman had another crew chief standing by the nitrogen cart readying the process. The crew chief Staff Sergeant (E-5), startled by my presence, ceased his preps to greet me as I told him to not yet resume the process. Meanwhile, all I could see were a set of legs standing in the nose wheel-well, maybe from the thighs down. I yelled up at him saying, "You need anything?" He said, "Yeah, another foot of hose. We're short and it won't reach the valve." I then tugged on the hose the opposite way and pissed him off. He yelled back, "The other way, asshole!" As I tugged again, he responded with familiar "F-expletives" of past times remembered. Really pissed, he crouched out of the wheel well, and saw my 8-striped shirt-sleeve with the hose in my hand ... as I gave his 3-stripes a stare (Senior Airman E-4).

As his jaw dropped, I noticed an "Oh shit" expression. I then looked at him in a stern manner and said, "As soon as you get off-duty tonight Airman, you will proceed to the Enlisted Club and meet me in the back bar where we shall have a serious chat ... and bring your servicing Sergeant who is guilty by association as your team mate, with you." As I departed, I could see the Master Sergeant shrug his shoulders and grin and told them, "Good luck at the Club. Merry Christmas!" So here they are, a few crew chiefs trying to close down the flight line, only to witness that event. They had a long day, I'm sure were tired, stinky, far from home for the holidays, and now demoralized looking forward to an ass-chewing from the Chief ... and there I was, waiting for them at the Tornado Alley Enlisted Club, with arms-crossed. In true form, I said to the one, "Airman, you were very disrespectful to me on that airplane tonight. As I contemplate what to do with you, I want to see you and your Sergeant eat these pizza slices and drink these draft beers. Go ahead. I've got all night."

So here they slowly chowed away on the pizza and beer as we looked at each other. I'm sure they were thinking that this Chief was, "Fattening them up for the kill," too. It was like 6 or 7 minutes as they tried to rapidly devour these two items as quickly as they could ... and I'm sure it felt like painful eternity as they couldn't imagine what was in my head during this process. Once they took their last swallows of beer and set their glasses down, I looked at them with a smile and said, "Great job tonight Airmen, you may be Chiefs someday. You each have another beer coming to you. Merry Christmas!" I then got up and went to the main bar and joined the Master Sergeant for a beer, as he witnessed what had just happened. He looked at me and said, "Chief, I'm sure there is a story behind this." I told him that it was a long journey of how a Cold War Airman became a post-Cold War Chief and of how it all began that snowy night in Bitburg 20 years ago ... now, a very heartfelt gratitude to that long ago Chief who would be pleased to know that I had continued his legacy. I would then move on to other assignments and other adventures beyond the Cold War.

Meanwhile, the post-Cold War climate was quite enjoyable. I would return to Altus to attend the inactivation ceremony of my old unit, the 57th Airlift Squadron and witness the last C-141B takeoff to retirement in July 2001. All four Altus aircraft performed a flyby. The C-5, C-17, and KC-135 gave C-141 tail number 50217 a wonderful sendoff, as I would once again watch another Cold War legend fly into the sunset (the Altus C-5As would follow the C-141s to AMARC later in 2007).

Ironically, my last assignment beckoned me back to one last existing Cold War platform that would not go away. In 2004, I would become the last Chief Enlisted Manager of the 4th Fighter Wing, 23rd Fighter Group at Pope Air Force Base, North Carolina. There were two fighter squadrons consisting of 43 Fairchild-Republic A-10A Thunderbolt II (Warthog) attacks jets that had kept very busy rotating in and out Iraq and Afghanistan, especially before and during the "Surge" years of 2005 through 2007. The A-10 was designed as a late 1970s Cold War "tank-killer" to take out the Soviet T-55, T-62, and T-72 tanks that were to attack west Europe from the Fulda Gap in Germany. The Warthogs were poised to do so and stationed in bases in England and Germany. The deterrence worked, the attack never came, and the Cold War ended.

But the A-10 continued service in South Korea and did extensive service during Desert Storm and its legacy continues. The famed teeth markings on the aircraft nose are from the 23rd Fighter Group's "Flying Tigers" that served in China and fought against the Japanese very early during the Second World War. With the "FT" on its tails, I was proud to be a part of that heraldry. Part of my Pope activity was closely associated with the 33 C-130's of the 43rd Airlift Wing that served on the same ramp. Many of those Cold War H models would depart by 2008 also.

To further add to my Cold War legacy, I would receive a unique request from headquarters Air Education and Training Command seeking a Cold War egress technician that had any affiliation to the Lockheed T-33 Shooting Star. The T-33 was produced in the late 1940s and 1950s and was America's first jet trainer. From 1953 to 1968 every Air Force pilot received advanced training in the aircraft. Over 6,550 "T-Birds" were built. It was retired from military service in 1971. But many were sold to foreign services and many became static displays and some put on pedestals across the country. Not too many records were kept by whoever took possession of them in the private sector. Over the years, The Air Force was trying to acquire some accountability and condition of these aircraft. One such airplane sat on a pedestal at the North Carolina Agricultural and Technical State University in Greensboro, North Carolina. It belonged to the Air Force Reserve Officer Training Corps (AFROTC) Detachment 605 – Home of the "Screaming Blackbirds" … screaming what? You guessed it. Their unit patch has an SR-71, in afterburner, on it. So, an old-timer at headquarters, seeing that unit logo, had remembered me, this old Cold War egress veteran, and had asked for a big favor before I retired.

You can imagine my expression when I was asked to go to a Greensboro college campus to open the canopy, verify that there were no live escape system explosive components, and to conduct radiation scans of the instrument panel components and gauges … I shook my head, wow!

So I gathered three A-10 crew chiefs with ladders and tools, and two bioenvironmental technicians from Pope and made the 1 ½ hour drive to Greensboro. The plane sat on top of a concrete pedestal with the canopy secured and rusted shut. The detachment commander had no real aircraft records except that the aircraft (tail number 061782) got washed from time to time.

The technical order that I received was an old schematic of how the canopy should open. But first, I was able to open an old external canopy jettison handle access door. The jettison lanyard was not there, thus, chances are, the explosive initiator was not in the cockpit either. To unlock the canopy, a breaker bar is inserted into an attachment point. It is then jimmied clockwise to rotate a torque tube that unlocks the canopy sill hooks, which forces the canopy to slide backward a few inches. This was no easy task as we used a few cans of spray lubricant to loosen up a few areas. Working with two ladders on each side of the canopy, we were able to unlock and retract the torque tubes. But to lift this big awkward canopy was a challenge. Normally this system has an electrical chain-driven motor, which may or may not be there, and probably was disconnected if it was there … I wouldn't trust putting any power to this aircraft anyway.

But we were able to slide small boards across the canopy sills then slide larger 2 x 4s to finally get the canopy erect enough to install a larger wooden support block to gain cockpit access. After determining the ejection seat and canopy system were without explosive components, the bioenvironmental crew suited up and activated their Geiger counter-type radiation scan measuring equipment. Turns out there were minimal traces of radiation with the few gauges that were there, but they were well within the safe zone. We closed down and secured the canopy, then briefly chatted with the detachment commander afterward.

We discussed the T-33 and the SR-71. He was so pleased to meet an actual SR-71 mechanic. I urged him to educate his students about the history of their logo aircraft and of the Cold War. The optics of watching this operation to the college campus students walking by must have been an intriguing sight to them. Hopefully, this old bird will raise questions among students to further inquire about it. As such, I had realized the Cold War story must be told. I am proud to have been able to share mine. And although this story ends with this T-33 episode and of my retirement in 2007, it is interesting to note, and how fitting it is, that I concluded the first draft writing of this book during the week of December 26, 2021 … the 30th anniversary of the end of the Cold War.

This Book Is Dedicated to the 148 Cold War Service Members Listed as Missing or Body Not Recovered
(Defense Pow-Mia Accounting Agency)

Cherished Retirement Items:

"Unseen Guardian" Sculpture, American Heroes, by Vanmark
& Sr-71 Signed Aircrew

EPILOGUE AND REFERENCES

The world would drastically change on September 11th, 2001 with the "9-11" attacks that would start the Global War on Terror … a far different challenge than the Global War on Communism that I had been used too. I would become involved and keep my hand in that fight until I eventually retired after 30 years of active duty in July of 2007. But during these years, other bits of Cold War history would surface as events and missions are declassified. Those battles of sovereign borders, territorial waters, and airspace were strictly monitored and responded too. Border security enforcement continued to be somewhat respected.

One such declassified mission is the story of an SR-71 from RAF Mildenhall (Det 4). It was 29 June 1987 during a routine flight to surveil Soviet activities in the Baltic Sea (although I supported such missions during my time at Det 4 in 1982, I did not realize how long these classified missions would continue, and would become known as "Baltic Express" missions). The aircraft blew one of its two engines near Soviet airspace which now made it a vulnerable target … it had lost speed and had to slowly descend. That meant it risked being shot down, forced to emergency land in not so friendly countries, or crash into the Baltic Sea. By now it had descended and violated Swedish air space and they were now being intercepted by two pairs of Swedish Air Force Saab 37 Viggen fighter jets. Although politically neutral during the Cold War (and never joined NATO) the Swedes visibly noticed that the Blackbird was in distress and escorted it to Danish airspace where F-15s from Bitburg, West Germany met, relieving the Viggen pilots. In turn, the F-15s then escorted the SR-71 to Nordholz Air Base in Denmark (a NATO member) where it safely landed. Unbeknownst to any of them at the time, one Soviet Mig-25 Foxbat pulled up a few miles to the left of the Viggens but observed and left the airspace. However, the National Security Agency (NSA) estimated that 20 Soviet aircraft had been launched. On 28 November 2018 in Stockholm, Sweden the U.S. Air Force presented the four Swedish pilots with Air Medals for "… deciding to render support to the aircraft by defending it from any potential third-party aircraft that might have tried to threaten it. The pilots then accompanied the aircraft beyond the territorial boundaries and ensured that it was safely recovered." It took declassifying this mission some 31 years later to finally recognize the airmanship of these pilots. That SR-71 easily was "MIG Bait" had the Viggens not fully escorted them to Denmark.

During the Cold War, May 1st, was known as "May Day." Known as "International Workers Day," it was an opportunity for Soviet bloc nations to show off their military hardware and missiles in parades. Leftist and Soviet-aligned regimes led by dictators would also show their might in public areas to display authority and force. I remember their blatant muscle-flexing on the newscast and the propaganda that would come from it. But their ideological alignment with other communists revealed how quickly those regimes turned into brutal dictatorships. It was also a reminder of the "Gulags" or labor camps that imprisoned political dissenters.

In 1985, there was a young Soviet Major in Dresden, East Germany who was working for the Soviet Union's agency of foreign intelligence and domestic security known as the KGB. His outpost was directly across the street from the East German Secret Police (Stasi). The Stasi monitored hundreds of thousands of citizens. As such, the KGB used the Stasi network to acquire intelligence and send it directly to Moscow. During this time of communist East Bloc authoritarianism and censorship, East Germany was a major focus of Moscow's attention because it was home to 380,000 Soviet troops and many Soviet intermediate range missiles. By 1989, this Soviet Major was promoted to Lieutenant Colonel and was still there when the communist East German regime collapsed amid mass pro-democracy protests. He returned to Russia and become the head of the Federal Security Service, the successor to the KGB. He would remember his Cold War experiences as he rose to higher positions in Russia. His name ... Vladimir Putin. (derived from "Putin's Career Rooted in Russia's KGB," David Hoffman, Washington Post Foreign Service, January 30, 2000, Page A1).

Less than two months after the 30th anniversary of the end of the Cold War, Vladimir Putin's Russia began a full-scale invasion of Ukraine. The largest conventional military attack in Europe since World War II. Although this is where my Cold War story ends, the Cold War legacy continues to this day ...

USAF Master Maintenance Badge (Wikimedia Commons)

Disclaimer: My memories are imperfect but I am sharing to the best of my knowledge and have changed identities where applicable. This story is a memoir based on my personal experiences from memory, photo albums, scrap books, diaries, airman performance reports (EPRs), and discussions with other friends and aircraft maintainers of the times.

Some references and information were derived from the following books and articles:

- Lockheed SR-71 Blackbird, Paul F Crickmore, 1986

- The Complete Book of the SR-71, Colonel Richard Graham, USAF, (Ret), 2015

- 50 Years of the U-2, The Complete Illustrated History of the Dragon Lady, Chris Pocock, 2005

- "Saving a Blackbird," Jennifer-Leigh Oprihory, Air Force Magazine, Jan-Feb 2019

- Iranian Aggression Ignites the 'Tanker War,' Mike Coppock, VFW Magazine, 1 April 2018

ECHOES AND WARNINGS FROM THE PAST....

"Freedom is never more than one generation away from extinction. We didn't pass it to our children through our bloodstream. It must be fought for, protected, and handed on for them to do the same."

Ronald Reagan

Remarks at Annual Convention of Kiwanis International – July 6, 1987

"The problem with socialism is that you eventually run out of someone else's money."

Margaret Thatcher

Speech to Conservative Party Conference, 10 October 1975

"Those who cannot remember the past are condemned to repeat it."

George Santayana

'The Life of Reason' 1905

"I can prophecy that your grandchildren in America will live under socialism – our firm conviction is that sooner or later Capitalism will give way to Socialism. Whether you like it or not, history is on our side. We will bury you."

Nikita Khrushchev

Speech to Western diplomats, Moscow, 18 November 1956

"The press is our chief ideological weapon."

Nikita Khrushchev

'The great mission of literature and art.' (1964)

"One, Socialism has never succeeded anywhere, including the Marxism-Leninism of the Soviet Union, the National Socialism of Nazi Germany, the Maoism of communist China, the Chavez-Maduro socialism of Venezuela. It has never come close anywhere to Marx's ideal of a classless society."

The Heritage Foundation, "THESE Are the Most Telling Failures of Socialism,"
Commentary by Lee Edwards, Ph.D., Distinguished Fellow in Conservative Thought, April 24, 2019

ABOUT THE AUTHOR

Chief Master Sergeant David Hamel retired after over 30 years of Air Force active duty service on 30 June 2007 as the last Chief Enlisted Manager of the 23rd Fighter Group: 4th Fighter Wing, 347th Rescue Wing, and 23rd Wing, at Pope AFB, NC. He served as the senior enlisted advisor to the commander on issues affecting the health, welfare, morale, training, development, and utilization of 925 enlisted airman that provided maintenance and munitions support to 43 A-10 aircraft and munitions support for five commands including 33 C-130 aircraft to meet mission taskings. He began his maintenance career as an Aircraft Egress (escape) Systems Specialist and progressed through supervisory and management positions on the F-15, U-2, TR-1, SR-71, B-52, FB-111, T-37, T-38, C-5, C-17, C-130, C-141, KC-135, and A-10 programs. He also performed special projects on the F-86, EB-57, AC-47, and T-33. He is a past Director of the Air Force Enlisted Heritage Research Institute and Enlisted Heritage Hall complex at the former College for Enlisted Professional Military Education, Air University, at Maxwell AFB, Alabama. He is an independent contractor supporting military special operations training in the Carolinas.

The Chief has an Associates in Applied Science degree in Aircraft Accessory Systems Technology through the Community College of the Air Force, an Associates degree in General Studies with Central Texas College, an Associate of Arts degree in Management, a Bachelor of Science degree in Technical Management with a secondary in Psychology with the University of Maryland, a Master of Arts degree in Computer Resources and Information Management and a Master of Arts degree in Human Resources Development, both with Webster University.

Chief Hamel is a Life Member of the Air Force Sergeants Association (AFSA) and has served two terms as a Trustee of AFSA's Airman Memorial Museum in Suitland, Maryland. He is also a Life Member of the Air Force Association and a charter sponsor of the Air Force Memorial in Washington DC. He is an All-State and All-American National Award Commander of the Veterans of Foreign Wars (VFW) Post 9103 Spring Lake, North Carolina. He is a past VFW POW-MIA Chairman for the Departments of Alabama and North Carolina, has performed 175 POW-MIA Remembrance programs, is a VFW National Aide-de-Camp and a former member of the National Scouting Team. He is also a past State Commander of the Alabama Korea Defense Veterans Association and has served as a Post Commander and Eastern District Commander of AMVETS North Carolina. He has life memberships with the Non-Commissioned Officers Association, American Legion, the Disabled American Veterans, and the VFW's Honor Degree - the Military Order of the Cootie, and is a former member of the American Legion's 40 & 8 Honor Society. He is also a 3rd and 4th degree member of the Knights of Columbus, a Catholic fraternal service organization.

The Chief is originally from Springfield, Massachusetts and currently resides in Spring Lake, North Carolina with his wife Gloria, of 28 years.

Ingram Content Group UK Ltd.
Milton Keynes UK
UKHW050759050723
424570UK00002B/23